D1438058

INTRODUCTION
TO THE DEVOUT LIFE

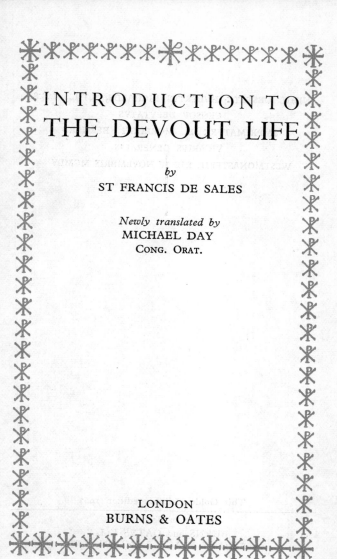

INTRODUCTION TO
THE DEVOUT LIFE

by

ST FRANCIS DE SALES

Newly translated by
MICHAEL DAY
CONG. ORAT.

LONDON
BURNS & OATES

NIHIL OBSTAT : HVBERTVS RICHARDS, S.T.L., L.S.S.
CENSOR DEPVTATVS
IMPRIMATVR : E. MORROGH BERNARD
VICARIVS GENERALIS
WESTMONASTERII: DIE IV NOVEMBRIS MCMLV

This Golden Library edition 1962

Printed in Belgium for
BURNS and OATES Ltd.
25 ASHLEY PLACE, LONDON, S.W.I.

TRANSLATOR'S NOTE

ST FRANCIS DE SALES was Bishop of Geneva from 1602 until his death twenty years later. In 1607, a certain Madame de Charmoisy, whose husband was an ambassador of the Duke of Savoy and a relative of St Francis, visited Annecy to attend to a lawsuit, and while there placed herself under his spiritual direction. When she returned to court he gave her a series of written spiritual instructions, which he had begun to compile as early as 1602, for the guidance of persons seeking to live a devout life in the world. These instructions were shown to Père Jean Fourier of the Society of Jesus, who considered them "a treasure of devotion", and so valuable that he strongly urged St Francis to have them printed, with the result that the first edition, edited by St Francis, was issued in 1609 under the title *Introduction à la Vie Dévote*.

He later thoroughly revised the work and added fresh material, the final edition being published in 1619. The following translation is from this text as established by Dom B. Mackey in the Annecy edition published in 1893.

Pius XI, in his Encyclical letter on the third centenary of the death of St Francis, refers to this book as "the most perfect of its kind" and expresses the wish that it be "read by all".

The present translation into simple, straightforward, contemporary English is an attempt to make this work of living devotion more widely accessible.

A translation into seventeenth-century English, or in an archaic style, would give it an air of unreality; too literal a translation would be no true translation and do no service to the original; on the other hand a certain freedom in translation might be mistaken for paraphrase.

The translator is concerned primarily with the thought of the original writer and with the problem of expressing that thought as clearly as possible; not only the words and phrases, but the very thought itself must be expressed in valid terminology; he is dealing with words as signs, and must use valid signs, signs which are valid here and now he must abandon signs which were once valid but are so no longer.

In the following work every effort has been made to use such valid terminology in a faithful and clear translation of an orginal which is indeed "a treasure of devotion".

MICHAEL DAY, CONG. ORAT.

The Oratory,
Edgbaston.
Feast of the Immaculate Conception, 1954.

CONTENTS

Contents

viii

Contents

ix

Contents

x

Contents

Contents

PREFACE

For your own satisfaction and for mine, please read this preface.

The flower girl Glycera was so skilful that by re-arranging her flowers she could make so many different bouquets that the painter Pausias, try as he might, could not capture their variety in his pictures.

In the same way, the Holy Spirit arranges the spiritual teaching which he puts before us through the tongues and pens of his servants with equal variety; the doctrines remain ever the same yet the manner in which they are presented differs according to the way they are arranged.

This *Introduction* contains nothing which has not already been written; the bouquet that I offer you is made up of the same flowers, but I have arranged them differently. Nearly everyone who has written about the spiritual life has had in mind those who live apart from the world, or at least the devotion they advocate would lead to such retirement. My intention is to write those who have to live in the world and who, according to their state, to all outward appearances have to lead an ordinary life; and who often enough, will not think of undertaking a devout life, considering it impossible; no one, they believe, ought to aspire to the palm of Christian piety while surrounded by the affairs of the world.

I will show them that a strong and resolute person may live in the world without being tainted by it, find spiritual springs amid its salt waters and fly through the flames of temptation without burning the wings on which they soar to God. True, it is no easy task and must be undertaken with much more zeal than many have so far shown, and I hope that this work will help those who undertake it with a generous heart.

This *Introduction* is not published entirely through my own choice or wish; an upright and virtuous person who, through the grace of God, aspired to a devout life, sought my help and, seeing how well disposed she was and being in many ways under an obligation to her, I set myself to do what I could.

Having led her through the suitable and necessary spiritual exercises, I left her some written notes to which she might refer. She later showed these notes to a wise and devout religious, who urged me to publish them, as he thought that they would be of great help to others. Because I valued his friendship and respected his judgement, I readily consented.

To make the whole work more presentable, I revised the notes and reduced them to some sort of order, adding various suitable pieces of advice, but I had to do this with very little leisure and so nothing has been treated at any great length; but what I have treated I have explained clearly and simply, at least that is what I have aimed at, but I have given no thought to style, as I have too much else to do.

My words are addressed to "Philothea", because it is a name signifying one who loves God, or at least desires to do so, and I have divided this *Introduction* into five parts.

In the first part I seek to lead Philothea from a simple desire for the devout life to a strong resolution to embrace it, making this resolution after a general confession, and following it up with Holy Communion, when she receives her Saviour, gives herself to him and enters into his love.

In the second part, I show her two great means by which she may unite herself more closely to him; the Sacraments, by which he comes to us; prayer, by which we unite ourselves to him.

In the third part, I show her how to practise the various virtues by which she will advance, concentrating on those points which she could not have discovered for herself or easily have found anywhere else.

In the fourth part, I show her some of the snares of the Enemy, how she may escape them and go forward.

In the last part, I make her go aside for a while to refresh herself, take breath and renew her strength for further progress in the devout life.

In a capricious age such as this, many will say that it is the task of religious and spiritual directors to guide individual souls on the way to devotion, that such a work requires more leisure than a bishop with a diocese as large as mine can well afford, and must prove a distraction from affairs of greater importance. I answer, however, with St Denis, that it belongs primarily to bishops to lead souls to perfection since their order is supreme among men as that of the seraphim is among the angels, so their leisure could never be more worthily employed.

The ancient bishops and fathers of the Church were no less assiduous than we are yet their epistles witness that they willingly guided individual souls who sought their aid, imitating the Apostles themselves who garnered with special care and affection certain outstanding grains of corn while harvesting the whole world; everyone knows that Timothy, Titus, Philemon, Onesimus, St Thecla and Appia were specially guided by St Paul, as

St Mark and St Petronilla were by St Peter (St Petronilla, as has been proved by Baronius and Galonius, being the spiritual daughter of St Peter, not his true daughter); and St John addressed one of his epistles to a devout woman named Electa.

To guide individual souls, I will admit, is exacting; but it is consoling work like that of the labourer in the vineyard, who is happiest when he has most to do. It is a work which refreshes the heart of those who undertake it, being a source of joy. A tigress, rescuing one of her young from the huntsman, feels it no burden, no matter how heavy it may be; love lightens her load and rather than hindering her it makes her swifter in her race for safety. How much more willingly then will a father take upon himself the charge of one who seeks holiness, carrying the burden as a mother her child upon her breast, never weary of bearing one whom she loves so much. It is true that one must have a fatherly heart for such a task and that is why the apostles called their disciples not only their children but, to show their tenderness, their *little* children.

It is true that I write about the devout life without being devout myself, though I certainly desire to be so, and it is my desire for devotion that encourages me to write. As a wise man once said, "To become learned it is good to study, better to have a learned master, but best of all to teach others." St Augustine, writing to Florentina, says: "To give disposes us to receive", so, to teach disposes us to learn.

Alexander commanded Apelles to paint the beautiful Campaspe whom he loved, and Apelles, gazing upon her while he carried out his work, found her image impressed upon his heart and became so much in love with her that Alexander, when he saw this, took pity on him and allowed him to marry her, depriving himself for the sake of Apelles of the woman he loved most; showing, as Pliny says, the greatness of his heart more clearly than had he won a mighty battle.

I am convinced that it is God's will that as a bishop I should paint upon men's hearts, not merely the ordinary virtues but above all that of devotion, which is the most pleasing in his sight, and I undertake the work most willingly, as much to fulfil my duty as to become more devout myself through imprinting this virtue on the hearts of others, and I hope that if ever God sees that I truly love devotion, he will give her to me in an eternal marriage.

The beautiful Rebecca, watering the camels of Isaac, was chosen to be his wife and she received as pledge golden earrings and bracelets; so I hope that while I am leading God's beloved sheep to the waters of devotion, he in his goodness will make my soul his own; place in my ears the golden words of his love, and on my arms the bracelets of his strength, that I may put those words into practice, for this is the essence of that true devotion which I beg God to bestow on me and upon all the children of his Church; to which Church I wish always to submit my writings, actions, words, desires . . . my every thought.

Annecy.
The Feast of St Mary Magdalen, 1609.

PART ONE

EMBRACING THE DEVOUT LIFE

I. TRUE DEVOTION

You seek devotion, Philothea, because you know, as a Christian, that this virtue is most pleasing to God.

Since slight mistakes in beginning any scheme are magnified as it progresses until they become almost irreparable, it is of prime importance that you know the exact nature of this virtue.

As there is only one true devotion while there are many imitations, unless you know how to recognize the true you may easily be decieved and waste your time in pursuit of what is merely false and superstitious.

Aurelius used to paint all the faces in his pictures in the image and likeness of the woman he loved, in the same way everyone depicts devotion according to his own liking and fancy.

One who is bent on fasting considers himself devout on this account even though his heart is full of bitterness. He fears to moisten his tongue with wine or even water, in the name of sobriety, yet does not hesitate to drink deep of his neighbour's blood by calumny and detraction.

Another thinks himself devout because he recites a great number of prayers every day, even though he follows this up by saying peevish, proud and hurtful things to those about him.

Another cheerfully opens his purse to give alms to the poor, yet will not open his heart to forgive his enemies; another will forgive his enemies yet will not pay his debts until forced to do so by the law. Such people are often considered devout though they certainly are not.

When Saul's servants were seeking David in his house, Michol dressed a statue in David's clothes and laid it on his bed so that they thought he was sick and asleep; in the same way many people clothe themselves in various externals of devotion which pass for the real thing when in fact they are no more than statues, mere phantoms of devotion.

Real living devotion, Philothea, presupposes the love of God; is in fact that very love, though it has many aspects. In so far as this love adorns the soul and makes us pleasing to God it is called grace; in so far as it empowers us to do good it is called charity; when it is so perfect that it moves us, not merely to do good, but to do good carefully, frequently and readily, then it is called devotion.

Ostriches never fly, hens fly sometimes but clumsily and not very high, but eagles, doves and swallows soar upwards swiftly and frequently.

In the same way sinners never fly towards God but travel on the earth seeking only earthly things. Those who are good but not yet devout do fly sometimes on the wings of good deeds, but slowly and ungracefully. Those who are devout soar on high to God frequently and readily.

In fact, then, devotion is nothing else but that spiritual alertness and vivacity which enables us to co-operate with charity promptly and wholeheartedly; and as it is the work of charity to make us keep generally and universally

7

all God's commandments, so it is the work of devotion to make us do so promptly and diligently. No one, then, who fails to keep God's commandments can be counted either good or devout, for to be good one must have charity while to be devout one must not only have charity but practise it cheerfully and with alacrity.

Since devotion is a high degree of charity it not only makes us ready, active and diligent in keeping God's commandments but also moves us to do as much good as we can vigorously and zealously, going beyond what is commanded to what is merely counselled or inspired.

A man who has recently recovered from some illness walks slowly and heavily and only as far as necessary. Similarly, a sinner who has just been healed of his iniquity walks slowly and heavily and only as far as God commands, until he attains to devotion. Then, like a man in sound health, he not only walks but runs and leaps in the way of God's commandments and beyond that in the path of heavenly counsels and inspirations.

In conclusion, then, charity is to devotion what the fire is to the flame, for charity is a spiritual fire which is called devotion when it breaks into flame, which, added to charity, makes it ready, active and diligent not only in keeping God's commandments but also in practising the heavenly counsels and inspirations.

2. THE VALUE OF DEVOTION

THOSE who discouraged the Israelites from entering the promised land told them that it was a country that *devoured its inhabitants*,[1] in other words, that the climate was so unhealthy that no one could live there for long,

[1] Num. 13. 33.

and that the inhabitants were such monsters that they devoured other men like locusts.

In the same way, Philothea, the world defames devotion as much as it can. The devout are represented with peevish, gloomy and sullen faces and devotion is said to make people melancholy and insupportable.

But as Josue and Caleb assured the Israelites that the promised land was good and fair and that the possession of it would be delightful and agreeable, so the Holy Spirit assures us through the saints, and our Lord himself assures us, that the devout life is pleasant, happy and agreeable.

The world sees that the devout fast, pray and bear injuries, serve the sick and give alms to the poor; it sees that they are vigilant, control their anger and their passions, deny themselves sensual pleasure and do many other things of their very nature difficult and austere; but what the world does not see is the interior devotion of the heart which makes them agreeable, pleasant and easy.

Look at the bees upon the thyme; they find there a very bitter juice but in sucking it they turn it into honey.

It is true that the devout find mortification bitter in itself, yet they convert this bitterness into sweetness when they practise it.

Fire and flame, wheel and sword seemed flowers and perfumes to the martyrs because they were devout; if devotion can make the most cruel torments, and even death, seem sweet, what will it do for the practice of virtue?

Sugar sweetens unripe fruit, and preserves from bitterness that which is ripe; devotion is, as it were, a spiritual sugar which sweetens mortification and makes consolations unharmful. It destroys discontent in the poor, anxiety in the rich, desolation in the oppressed and arrogance in the exalted; it takes away unhappiness from those who are alone and dissipation from those in company.

It is as fire in winter and dew in summer; it knows how to meet with riches and want, how to turn to profit both honour and contempt, and renders the heart constant in face both of pleasure and of pain, filling us with a wonderful delight.

Jacob's ladder is a true image of the devout life, the two sides between which we climb represent prayer which obtains the love of God and the sacraments which confer it, the rungs represent the various degrees of charity by which we go from virtue to virtue, descending by the practice of charity to our neighbour or ascending by contemplation to loving union with God.

If we look at those on the ladder we see that they are either men with angelic souls or angels with human bodies; though not young they seem so, being full of vigour and spiritual agility; they have wings to soar up to God by prayer yet feet to walk among men, edifying them by their holiness.

They have beautiful and cheerful faces because they receive all things with happiness and contentment.

Their legs and arms and heads are uncovered because all they think and feel and do is unencumbered by any other thought than that of pleasing God.

The rest of their body is covered with a beautiful light robe to show that they do make use of earthly things but only of what is really necessary, using with moderation what befits their state. Such are the devout.

Believe me, Philothea, devotion is delightful above

all else, and the queen of virtues because the perfection of charity; it is to charity as cream to milk, as the flower to the plant, as lustre to a precious stone or as the perfume to precious balm, it is the odour of sweetness which comforts men and rejoices the angels.

3. DEVOTION SUITABLE TO ALL

AT the creation God commanded the plants to bear fruit each according to its kind and he likewise commands Christians, the living branches of the vine, to bear fruit by practising devotion according to their state in life.

The practice of devotion must differ for the gentleman and the artisan, the sevant and the prince, for widow, young girl or wife. Further, it must be accommodated to their particular strength, circumstances and duties.

Is the solitary life of a Carthusian suited to a bishop? Should those who are married practise the poverty of a Capuchin? If workmen spent as much time in church as religious, if religious were exposed to the same pastoral calls as a bishop, such devotion would be ridiculous and cause intolerable disorder.

Such faults are however very common; and the world, which cannot or will not distinguish between true devotion and the indiscretions of the self-styled devout, blames and criticizes devotion itself as responsible for those disorders.

True devotion, Philothea, never causes harm, but rather perfects everything we do; a devotion which conflicts with anyone's state of life is undoubtedly false.

Aristotle tells us that the bee sucks honey from the flowers without injuring them, leaving them as whole and fresh as when it found them. Devotion goes further, not only is it unharmful to any state of life, it adorns and beautifies it.

It makes the care of a family peaceful, the love of a husband and wife more sincere, the service of one's king more faithful, and every task more pleasant and a joy.

It is not only erroneous, but a heresy, to hold that life in the army, the workshop, the court, or the home is incompatible with devotion.

True, Philothea, monastic or religious devotion cannot be practised in these callings; yet these are not the only kinds of devotion; there are many others suitable for those who live in the world and capable of leading them to perfection.

Under the old law, the lives of Abraham, Isaac, Jacob, David, Job, Tobias, Sara, Rebecca and Judith are a proof of this. Under the new law, St Joseph, Lydia and St Crispin were perfectly devout in the workshop; St Anne, St Martha, St Monica, Aquila, Priscilla in their homes; Cornelius, St Sebastian, St Maurice in the army; Constantine, Helen, St Louis, Blessed Amadeus and St Edward in the courts. It has even happened that many have fallen away in solitude, in itself so conducive to perfection, and preserved their virtue in the midst of crowds, which are unconducive to it, as happened in the case of Lot who, as St Gregory says, lost in solitude the chastity he had so well preserved in the city. No, Philothea, wherever we find ourselves we not only may, but should, seek perfection.

4. THE NECESSITY OF A GUIDE

WHEN young Tobias, commanded to go to Rages, said: "I do not know the way", his father told him to find someone to guide him; and if you wish to walk the path of devotion, Philothea, I say the same to you: find someone to guide you. It is the most important advice I can offer you. Blessed John of Avila tells us that this humble obedience, so much recommended and practised by the saints, is the surest way to find the will of God.

St Teresa wished to imitate the rigorous penances of Catherine of Cardona, and when her confessor forbade her to do so she was tempted to disobey until God said to her, "My daughter, your way is good and safe; I value your obedience higher than her penance." This gave her such a love for obedience that over and above the obedience she owed to her superiors she made a special vow to follow the advice and guidance of her confessor; a practice which brought her great consolation.

The same is true of many others who have submitted their will to God's servants the more surely to submit themselves to him.

St Catherine of Siena recommends such obedience in her *Dialogues*; the devout princess St Elizabeth practised entire obedience to the learned Master Conrad; before his death St Louis counselled his son, "Confess often; choose a good and wise confessor, who can teach you safely what you must do."

A faithful friend, says Holy Scripture, *is a strong defence, and he that hath found him hath found a treasure. A faithful friend is the medicine of life and of immortality, and they that fear the Lord shall find him.*[1] You will notice that these divine words refer principally to *immortality* and to the necessity of a *faithful friend* to guide us there by his counsel and advice, and to be a *strong defence* against the snares and deceptions of the devil.

[1] Ecclus. 6. 14-16.

13

In our troubles, sorrows and failures he will be a *treasure* of wisdom; in our spiritual sickness he will be a *medicine* to ease and console our hearts; he will preserve us from evil and turn our good to better; and if we should fa llhe will rescue us, ensuring that it is not fatal.

Who shall find such a friend? The wise man answers *they that fear the Lord*, in other words, those who are humble and sincerely desire to progress towards holiness.

Since it is so very important, Philothea, that you travel with a good guide, implore God to send you one after his own Heart, and be sure that he who sent an angel from heaven to guide Tobias will send someone good and faithful to guide you; one whom in fact, when you have found him, you should look on as an angel, not merely as a man.

Do not place your trust in him as though he were no more than man, nor in his merely human knowledge, but trust God, who will speak to you and grant graces through him. God will put into his heart and on his lips whatever is necessary for your happiness. Listen to him, then, as though he were an angel from heaven sent to guide you there.

Open your heart to him truthfully and sincerely, tell him everything good and bad, hide nothing and pretend nothing, in this way the good will be examined and made more sure and the bad corrected and remedied; you will be comforted and strengthened in time of trouble, moderated and restrained in time of prosperity.

Have every confidence in him, together with a holy reverence; a reverence not diminished by your confidence and a confidence not hindered by your reverence; in other words, let your confidence be full of filial respect so that your relationship may be strong, sacred, entirely spiritual and divine.

That this may be possible, Avila tells us, we should choose one in a thousand, and I say, one in ten thousand, for those fitted for such a task are unimaginably few.

He must be full of charity, knowledge and prudence; if he lacks any of these qualities there is danger.

However, I say again, pray for such a man and bless God when you find him; then remain constant and seek no further but go forward in simplicity, humility and confidence, for your journey will be attended with every success.

5. THE PURIFICATION OF THE SOUL

At home the flowers have begun to blossom, pruning time has come.[1] The flowers of our heart, Philothea, are good desires. As soon as they appear we must take a pruning-knife and cut away all dead and superfluous works. Before marrying an Israelite, an alien girl had to *lay aside the garb of a captive, shave her head and pare her nails close.*[2] Similarly those who aspire to the honour of being a spouse of Christ must *put off the old man, and put on the new,*[3] forsaking sin, then pare down and shave away whatever hinders union with God.

The first step to health is the purgation of bad dispositions. St Paul was perfectly cleansed in an instant, as were St Catherine of Genoa, St Mary Magdalen, St Pelagia and many others; but such purification is as extraordinary and miraculous in the order of grace, as re-

[1] Cant. 2 12   [2] Deut. 21 12   [3] Eph 4 22

surrection from the dead in the order of nature, and so we cannot rely on that.

Normally the purification and healing of mind or body is a gradual process, brought about step by step with effort and patience.

The angels on Jacob's ladder had wings, yet instead of flying they ascended and descended in an orderly way from one step to another.

The transition from sin to devotion is like the coming of the dawn, the darkness is only dispelled gradually; the slowest cure is the surest. The ills of the soul, like those of the body, come post-haste on horseback and depart slowly, on foot, so, Philothea, this enterprise demands patience and courage.

How sad it is that so many, after practising devotion for a while, become anxious, troubled and discouraged at finding themselves still imperfect, so much so that they almost yield to the temptation to give up everything and return to their old ways!

On the other hand, how dangerous the opposite temptations to think themselves delivered from their imperfections as soon as they begin; to think that they are already perfect and to try to fly before they are fledged! In how great danger of falling way, Philothea, are those who leave the doctor's hands too soon!

The Psalmist tells us not to rise *before the light is come*, but to *rest awhile* before we *stir abroad;*[1] and he put his advice into practice, for having been already washed and cleansed, he prayed that he might be *washed yet more.*[2]

The task of purifying the soul cannot, may not, end as long as we live; however, our imperfections should not

[1] Ps. 126 2   [2] Ps. 50. 4.

make us anxious, for perfection consists in fighting against them, and we cannot fight them unless we see them, or overcome them if we do not face up to them.

Victory does not lie in being unconscious of them, it lies in not consenting to them, and we are not consenting to them as long as they displease us.

In fact, to learn humility, we must sometimes be wounded in this spiritual warfare, but we will never be defeated unless we lose courage or our life, and as our spiritual life is lost only by mortal sin never by imperfection or venial sins, we have only to look to our courage, praying with David that God may rescue us from the fears that daunt us and from the storm around us.[1]

Luckily, in this kind of battle, we shall always be victorious as long as we are prepared to fight.

6. PURIFICATION FROM MORTAL SIN

PURIFICATION from mortal sin is the first step, and the sacrament of penance is the means of effecting it. Seek the best confessor you can; make use of some book designed to help us to make a good confession, by, for example, Granada, Bruno, Arias, Auger. Go through it carefully, noting, point by point, where you have offended from the time you came to the use of reason up to the present; writing it down if you distrust your memory.

Having discovered and noted the sins which beset your consience, detest them and renounce them with all the sorrow and contrition in your heart, remembering these four points: that by sin you have lost the grace of God; that you have forfeited your place in heaven; that you

[1] Cf. Ps. 54.9.

have deserved the eternal suffering of hell and that you have renounced the eternal love of God.

You will notice, Philothea, that I advocate a general confession of your whole life, though I freely admit that this is not strictly necessary; however, I regard it as most useful at the beginning and so strongly advise it.

The ordinary confessions of those who live in the world are often very defective owing to lack of preparation or of contrition, if not through an implicit intention of falling again, for some are unwilling to avoid the occasions of falling again, for some are unwilling to avoid the occasions of sin or to take the means necessary to amend their life. In such cases a general confession is necessary to make our soul secure; while in addition it enables us to know ourselves better, stirs up a healthy shame for our past, and awakens wonder at God's mercy in bearing with us for so long. It tranquillizes our heart, calms our mind and stirs us up to good resolutions; it gives our confessor the chance to advise us suitably, and gives us greater confidence in unburdening our heart for the future.

Since I am speaking of a general reformation of heart and the complete conversion of your soul to God by embracing the devout life, I think it is wise, Philothea, to advise a general confession.

7. PURIFICATION FROM ATTACHMENT TO MORTAL SIN

THOUGH all the Israelites left Egypt, some were still attached to it and so repined for the fleshpots of Egypt. In the same way many penitents give up their sins but are still attached to them. They promise not to sin again but give up the uneasy pleasure of sin only with reluctance; their heart has turned from sin and left it behind yet they often look back as Lot's wife looked back at Sodom. They abstain from sin as a sick man abstains from melon, with great reluctance and only because the doctor tells him it would be fatal; he talks about it and is unwilling to believe it harmful; he likes to smell it and envies those who eat it.

It is the same with weak and lukewarm penitents, they would be very happy if they could sin without being damned; they speak of sin as of something regretfully lost, and of sinners as though theirs were the happier lot.

A man who has turned away from thoughts of revenge in confession may soon afterwards be found bragging of his quarrel to his friends, saying what he would have done but for his fear of God; that the divine law in the matter of forgiveness is hard and that it is a pity that revenge is not allowed.

It is obvious that though he has turned from sin he is still very much attached to it; he has left Egypt yet his heart is still there, yearning for the garlic and onions which were once his delight. It is the same with a woman who has given up her love affairs and yet still being flattered and courted. Such people are certainly in grave danger.

If you desire to embrace the devout life, Philothea, you must not only give up sin but also free your heart from all attachment to it, for such attachment not only places you in danger of relapsing but is a constant source of weakness and discouragement, preventing you from doing good readily, diligently and frequently, which is the essence of devotion.

Those who are still subject to such weakness after

turning from sin are like anaemic girls, who though not sick act as though they were, eating without relish, sleeping without repose, laughing without joy and walking with heavy step; for they do good with such weariness of spirit that they effect little and what they do effect lacks all vitality.

8. THE MEANS TO THIS PURIFICATION

THE first step towards this purification is a clear and vivid realization of the terrible effects of sin, leading to sincere and vehement contrition.

As even weak contrition, so long as it is sincere, cleanses us from sin, especially through the power of the sacraments, so a deep and vehement contrition cleanses us from even attachment to it.

Any dislike or bitter feeling towards anyone causes us to avoid him; but a deadly and violent hatred causes us not only to avoid him, but also everyone and everything connected with him, his family, friends, possessions, even this portait. In the same way when a penitent's renunciation of sin is based on weak, though sincere, contrition, he is merely resolved to sin no more; but when his contrition is strong and vigorous, he not only detests sin but its occasions, and everything connected with it.

It follows then, Philothea, that we must extend our contrition as far as possible to embrace everything connected with sin, as was the case with Mary Magdalen, who so lost her attachments to her sins when she was converted that she never even thought of them again; and also with David, who renounced not only sin but all the ways and paths that led to it. Such conversion is the re-birth of the soul which David compares to the restoration of the eagle's plumage.[1]

To obtain such perfect contrition you must carefully make the following meditations which, with the help of God's grace, will enable you to root out from your heart both sin and your main attachments to it, for such was my purpose in composing them.

Follow them in the order set out, taking only one a day, preferably in the morning, as being the most suitable time for spiritual exercises, and then turn the matter over in your mind during the rest of the day.

If you are not yet accustomed to meditation read what is said about it in Part Two.

9. FIRST MEDITATION: OUR CREATION

Preparation

Place yourself in the presence of God and ask him to inspire you.

Considerations

1. Consider that a few years ago you were not in the world at all, that you were nothing. O my soul, where was I then? The world had already lasted so long and I was not known.

2. God has raised you from this nothingness and made you what you are purely out of his goodness, for he had no need of you.

3. Consider what nature God has given you; the highest in the visible world, capable of eternal life and perfect union with himself.

[1] Ps. 102. 5.

21

Spiritual Acts and Resolutions

1. Humble yourself profoundly before God, saying from your heart with the Psalmist: *O Lord, I am as nothing before thee. Why hast thou been mindful of me to create me?*[1] Oh my soul, I was in an abyss of nothingness and would still be there had not God drawn me thence; and still there what could I have done?

2. Give thanks to God. O my great and good Creator, how much I owe to thee who in thy mercy hast willed to raise me from my nothingness to make me what I am. What can I possibly do to bless thy name worthily or thank thee enough for thy inestimable goodness?

3. Abase yourself. Alas, my Creator, instead of uniting myself to thee by loving service, my inordinate desires have made me a rebel and I have cut myself off from thee by preferring sin, dishonouring thee as though thou wert not my Creator.

4. Cast yourself down before God, *Know*, my soul, *that the Lord is thy God*: he made thee; thou didst not make thyself. O God, *I am the work of they hands.*[2]

5. From now on I will no longer exalt myself, for by myself I am nothing. What have I to glory in who am but dust and ashes, and even less than that! What have I to be proud of?

In order to humble myself I will take the means necessary, bear with humiliations, and change my life. I will follow my Saviour, honouring the nature he has granted me, according to his will, in obedience, under the guidance of my spiritual director.

Conclusion

1. *Thanksgiving. Bless thy God, O my soul, and let all*

[1] Ps. 38. 7; 8. 5. [2] Ps. 99. 3.

that is within me bless his holy name,[1] for in his goodness he has lifted me from nothingness and in his mercy created me.

2. *Offering.* O my God, with all my heart I offer thee the being thou hast given me; I dedicate and consecrate it to thee.

3. *Petition.* Strengthen me, O God, in these desires and resolutions. O Blessed Virgin, recommend them to the mercy of thy Son.

Our Father. Hail Mary.

Your prayer completed, wander back in spirit among your considerations and gather a bouquet of spiritual thoughts to perfume your whole day.

10. SECOND MEDITATION: WHY WE WERE CREATED

Preparation

Place yourself in the presence of God and ask him to inspire you.

Considerations

1. God has not placed you in the world because he needs you, for you are useless to him, but simply to manifest his goodness in you by giving you his grace and glory; and to this end has given you an intellect to know him, a memory to remember him, a will to love him, an imagination to represent to yourself his benefits, eyes to look upon the wonder of his works, a tongue to speak his praise. . . and so of your other faculties.

2. Since you were created and put in the world for this end you must reject and avoid any actions which

[1] Ps. 102. 1.

23

lead you away from it, and count as vain and useless those which lead you no nearer.

3. Consider the wretchedness of worldly people who never think of their true purpose, but live as though they were created only to build houses, plant trees, amass riches and amuse themselves.

Spiritual Acts and Resolutions

1. Reproach yourself humbly for your wretchedness in never having thought of these things before. What was I thinking about, my God, when not of thee? What was I remembering when I was forgetful of thee? Where was my heart when not set upon thee? Truth should have been my food and yet I gorged myself with vanity, serving the world created to serve me.

2. Detest your past life. Vain thoughts and useless reasonings, I turn from you; hateful and empty memories, I renounce you; faithless and false friendships, harmful and wretched habits, selfish pleasure and unhappy indulgences, I will have no part with you.

3. Turn to God. My God and my Saviour, from now on I will think only of thee; no more of things which may displease thee. My memories shall be ever of thy greatness and thy mercy so tenderly exercised on me. My heart shall find all its delight in thee and thou shalt be the object of its love. From now on I will detest the useless follies which have occupied my days and all the useless objects of my love, and accordingly amend my life.

Conclusion

1. *Thanksgiving.* Thank God for having created you for so high a destiny. Thou hast made me for thyself, O Lord, that I may rejoice forever in the immensity of thy

glory. Thy glory! When shall I be worthy of it? When shall I bless thee as I ought?

2. *Offering*. I offer thee, my Creator, these spiritual acts and resolutions with all my heart and soul.

3. *Petition*. Accept, O God, these desires and aspirations and give me thy blessing that I may put them into practice through the merits of thy Son who shed his blood for me upon the cross.

Gather your bouquet of thoughts.

II. THIRD MEDITATION: THE BENEFITS OF GOD
Preparation

Place yourself in the presence of God and ask him to inspire you.

Considerations

1. Consider the bodily gifts which God has showered on you. Your body, the abundant means to keep it alive, its lawful pleasures and comforts, your friends, so many things to help you. Compare your own case with that of so many others who are more worthy and who have yet been denied them: those who are disabled, maimed and ill, those who have no friends, who are despised and dishonoured, or suffering poverty. God has spared you these miseries.

2. Consider your gifts of mind. Many people are half-witted, mad or insane, yet you are not of their number; God has treated you with favour. Similarly, many have had no upbringing and are ignorant, yet Divine Providence has granted you a good education in every way.

3. Consider your spiritual gifts. You are a child of the Church, Philothea. From childhood God has taught

you about himself. He has given his sacraments so often and his interior graces and aspirations, awakening your conscience. He has pardoned your sins, and delivered you from the dangers which beset your soul. What have all these years been but an opportunity to grow in grace? Consider these things one by one and you will realize how gracious and tender God has been to you.

Spiritual Acts and Resolutions

1. Wonder at God's goodness. How good God is to me, how good he is in himself; thy heart, O Lord, is rich in mercy and abounding in love. Forever I will sing of thy favours to me.

2. Wonder at your ingratitude. *What am I, Lord, that thou art mindful of me?*[1] How unworthy I am! I have trodden thy benefits under foot; abused thy graces and denied thy goodness by rejecting them. I have opposed the abyss of my ingratitude to the abyss of the grace and goodness.

3. Awaken your gratitude. Be no longer faithless, my heart; no longer ungrateful and disloyal to your great benefactor. *Shall not my soul henceforth be subject to God*[2] who has worked such wonders of grace in and for me?

4. Detach your heart, Philothea, from its false pleasures and consecrate it to God who has done so much for it. Apply your soul to knowing him and thanking him in ways best suited to your state. Make careful use of the means offered by the Church to save your soul and to love God.

I will be faithful to prayer, receive the sacraments often, listen to the word of God and put into practice his inspirations and counsels.

[1] Ps. 8. 5.　　[2] Ps. 61. 1.

Conclusion

1. *Thanksgiving.* Thank God for making your duty known, and for all the graces he has so far granted you.

2. *Offering.* Offer him your heart and your resolutions.

3. *Petition.* Pray for the strength to keep to them through the merits of his Son and ask our Lady and the saints to intercede for you.

Our Father. Hail Mary.

Gather your bouquet of thoughts.

12. FOURTH MEDITATION: SIN

Preparation

Place yourself in the presence of God and ask him to inspire you.

Considerations

1. Consider how long it is since you began to sin, how sin has multiplied in your heart, increasing day by day; sins against God, against those about you, by word and deed, by thought and desire.

2. Consider your evil inclinations and how far you have followed them. You will conclude that your *sins are countless as the hairs on your head,*[1] more numerous than the grains of sand on the seashore.

3. Consider alone the sin of ingratitude to God, a sin so fundamental that it affects all your sins and makes them very much worse. Consider all God's many benefits and how you have used them against him, inspirations neglected, graces rejected. Consider how often you have received the sacraments and where is the fruit? Where

[1] Ps. 39. 13.

27

are the precious jewels with which he adorned your soul? They are buried beneath your sins. What preparation have you made before receiving the sacraments?

What ingratitude to lose yourself fleeing from him who seeks you only to save you.

Spiritual Acts and Resolutions

1. Be ashamed of your wretchedness. How dare I appear before thee, my God, when I am but refuse, a sink of ingratitude and iniquity? What disloyalty! No single sense, no faculty of soul not abused and defiled no single day free from such evils. What a return for thy graces; for the blood of my Saviour!

2. Ask forgiveness. Cast yourself at our Lord's feet, as a prodigal son, as another Magdalen, or as a woman who has defiled her marriage-bed with sins of adultery. O God, have pity on me a sinner, O fountain of mercy, pity me in my misery.

3. Resolve to change your life. With the help of thy grace, O my God, I will never again surrender to sin. I now detest what I have loved only too well, and turn to thee, Merciful Father, resolved to live and die in thee.

4. To blot out my past sins I will confess them courageously and cast every one of them from my soul.

5. I will do all I can to destroy their roots in my heart, especially those which have troubled me most.

6. To do this I will constantly take the means recommended to me, and never think that I have done enough to make reparation for such serious offences.

Conclusion

1. *Thanksgiving.* Thank God for waiting so patiently for you till now, and for giving you these good desires.

2. *Offering*. Offer him your heart that you may put them into practice.

3. *Petition*. Pray for strength to do so.

13. FIFTH MEDITATION: DEATH

Preparation

1. Place yourself in the presence of God and ask him to give you his grace.

2. Imagine yourself on your death-bed incurably ill.

Considerations

1. Consider the uncertainty of the day of your death. One day, my soul, you must depart from this body. When will it be? In winter or summer? In town or country? During the day or night? With or without warning? As the result of illness or accident? Shall I have a chance to go to confession? Shall I be assisted by a priest? Unhappily I know none of these things; only one thing is certain, I will die, and sooner than I imagine.

2. Consider that then the world will come to an end as far as you are concerned. You will have no more part in it. It will turn upside down before your eyes, for worldly joys and pleasure and the things you loved in vain will turn into empty dreams and shadows.

Fool that I am to offend God for the sake of such trifling vanities. I have forsaken God for nothing!

On the other hand, devotion and good deeds will be seen as desirable and delightful and you will ask yourself: Why did I not walk by this beautiful and pleasant path?

At that hour your sins, which at the time seemed so small, will appear as big as mountains and your devotion truly very small.

3. Consider how reluctantly your soul will bid farewell to this world, to its riches and vanities, to worldly company and pleasures, to amusements, friends, family, to everything, and last of all your own body, leaving it pale, wasted away, hideous and fearful.

4. Consider how your body will be hurried to the grave and then the world will give no more thought to you than you have given to others. They will say "God rest his soul" and that will be the end of it. Such is the pitiless power of death.

5. Consider the destination of your soul once it has left the body. In which direction will it go? It will continue in the same direction as on earth!

Spiritual Acts and Resolutions

1. Pray to God and cast yourself into his arms. Take me into thy care on that awful day; may all my other days be sad if only that may be a happy one.

2. Despise the world. Since I do not know when I will part from the world I will not be attached to it. No love for friends or relatives save what is holy, save what can last forever; for why should I love them with a love which death can end?

3. I will prepare for that hour and ensure that it may be a happy one. I will do all I can to make my conscience clear and resolve to overcome all my shortcomings.

Conclusion

Thank God for inspiring these resolutions and offer them to him, imploring him to give you a happy death

through the merits of his Son, through the intercession of our Lady and the saints.
Our Father, Hail Mary.
Gather your bouquet of thoughts.

14. SIXTH MEDITATION: FINAL JUDGEMENT

Preparation

Place yourself in the presence of God and ask him to inspire you.

Considerations

1. At the appointed time after many dreadful signs and portents at which men will wither away for fear and expectation, a torrent of fire will reduce the earth to ashes sparing nothing.

2. Then everyone shall rise from the grave save those already risen and, at the voice of the Archangel, gather in the Valley of Josaphat. What differences however! Some will have glorious and radiant bodies, others hideous and repellent ones.

3. Consider the Majesty of the Judge when he appears attended by the saints and angels, his Cross before him shining like the sun, a symbol of mercy for the good and of justice for the wicked.

4. At his command the good and wicked will be separated, the good on his right, the wicked on his left, separated forever, never to meet again.

5. Then will all consciences be manifested, the sins and ingratitude of the wicked, the repentance and graces of the good, nothing being hidden; the wicked shall be confounded and the good consoled.

6. Consider the final sentence of the wicked. *Go far from me, you that are accursed, into the eternal fire which has been prepared for the devil and his angels.*[1] Try to realize how terrible these words are. *Go far from me.* A sentence of everlasting banishment from his presence; then, to be called *accursed* by God is the most terrible and final of all maledictions, and an eternal one for he adds *into eternal fire*; an eternity of suffering; nothing could be more terrible.

7. Consider on the other hand what he will say to the good, drawing them to his heart, the source of all goodness. *Come, you who have received a blessing from my Father* (to be blessed of the Father is to receive all blessings); *take possession of the kingdom which has been prepared for you since the foundation of the world*[2] (the crown of all blessings, for this kingdom shall have no end).

Spiritual Acts and Resolutions

1. Remember these things, my soul, and tremble. Who can save me, my God, on the day when the very *pillars of heaven*[3] tremble with fear?

2. Detest your sins which alone will stand against you on that awful day.

3. I will judge myself now that I may not be judged then; examine my conscience, condemn myself and amend my ways that the Judge may not condemn me on that dread day. To this end I will go to confession and take all the means necessary.

Conclusion

1. *Thanksgiving*. Thank God for giving you the means of preparing for that day, and time for penance.

[1] Matt. 25. 41.   [2] Matt. 25.34.   [3] Job 26.11.

2. *Offering.* Offer him your heart to this end.

3. *Petition.* Ask him to give you the grace to take these means.

Our Father. Hail Mary.

Gather your bouquet of thoughts.

15. SEVENTH MEDITATION: HELL

Preparation

1. Place yourself in the presence of God and humbly ask his help.

2. Imagine yourself in a city of gloom, a city of burning pitch and brimstone, a city whose inhabitants can never escape.

Considerations

1. Like those in this city, the damned are in the depths of hell, suffering unspeakable torments in every sense and member; having used their life to sin they suffer pain befitting their sin; eyes which looked on evil things will endure the awful vision of devils and of hell; ears which delighted to hear evil conversations will listen for ever to wailings and lamentation and cries of despair.

2. Yet greater than all these torments is the loss of the glory of God, being deprived for ever of the sight of it. If Absalom found the suffering of never seeing his father's face greater than that of banishment, how much greater our suffering at being excluded for ever from the face of God!

3. Consider that what makes hell intolerable is the fact that our suffering can never have an end. If a little tickle in your ear or a slight fever makes the night seem endless, how terrible that eternal night when afflicted with

so many sufferings! An eternal night which gives birth
to eternal despair and frenzied blasphemies without end.

Spiritual Acts and Resolutions

1. Stir your soul to terror. Could I endure *the devour-
ing flame... of fires that burn unceasingly*? [1] Am I really prepared to cut myself off for ever from God?

2. I must admit that I have often deserved such a fate,
yet why should I go down to the abyss? From now on I
will travel away from it.

3. To this end I will take all possible means to avoid
sin, which alone can lead me to that everlasting death.
Conclude as before.

16. EIGHTH MEDITATION: HEAVEN

Preparation

Place yourself in the presence of God and ask his help.

Considerations

1. Think of the beauty of a clear night sky and of the
wonder of its countless different stars; then of the beauty
of a lovely day, and imagine that the radiance of the sun
in no way dims the beauty of the stars and moon; such
loveliness cannot compare with that of heaven; how lovely it must be, how precious, how desirable.

2. Consider the radiant nobility of that country's
countless citizens; angels, cherubim and seraphim;
apostles, martyrs and confessors; virgins and holy women such a multitude and such happiness; the least of
them more beautiful than all the world; what happiness
to gaze on them. Eternal love is ever the burden of their

[1] Isa. 33. 13.

song; unfailing joy fills their hearts; a joy beyond compare which they communicate to one another in a blissful union which can never have an end.

3. Consider lastly their happiness in enjoying God, who favours them for ever with his visible presence and fills their hearts with all delight.

What joy to be one with the fountainhead of their very being!

Like birds singing for joy they wing their way through the air of God's encompassing divinity and its unbelievable delights; vying with one another in singing his praises, yet without envy.

O my Creator my Saviour, I bless thee for thy liberality in granting eternally the treasure of thy glory.

And God replies, "Be blessed for ever, my beloved children, who have served me and who will praise me so lovingly and so fervently for all eternity."

Spiritual Acts and Resolutions

1. Admire and praise this beautiful country. Jerusalem, how beautiful thou art; how happy thine inhabitants!

2. Reproach yourself for cowardice in so often falling away from the path to this glorious abode.

Why have I strayed so far from the path to my greatest happiness? For the sake of vain and empty pleasures I have turned my back a hundred times upon eternal and ineffable delights. What madness to despise them for desire of empty vanities.

3. Set your whole heart upon heaven. Since thou hast directed me once more into thy ways, O Lord, I will never turn aside again but go forward to eternal rest; to that promised land of blessedness, this Egypt no more my resting place.

4. I will cast off everything which holds me back upon my journey there, and do all I can to reach my goal.

Conclude as before.

17. NINTH MEDITATION: CHOICE OF HEAVEN

Preparation

Place yourself in the presence of God and humbly ask him to inspire you.

Considerations

Imagine yourself on an open plain, alone with your guardian angel, like Tobias on the way to Rages, and imagine that he shows you heaven open above you and all the joys we have already considered; then imagine that he shows you hell open below you with all the sufferings described in the meditation on hell. With this choice before you and kneeling at his feet:

1. Consider that you are in reality between heaven and hell and that according to your choice one or the other will be your end.

2. Consider that the choice you make in this world will last for ever in the next.

3. Although both are open to you according to your choice, God, who is ready to give you either the first by his mercy or the second by his justice, desires above all else that you should choose heaven; and your guardian angel is doing all he can to obtain for you every possible help to bring you there.

4. Jesus Christ looks down with mercy from heaven and says to you, "Come, seek eternal rest within my arms; come and enjoy the everlasting happiness which, in the abundance of my love, I have prepared for thee",

then turn your eyes to our Lady who, with maternal love, says to you, "Have courage; do not despise my ardent prayers nor the desires of my Son, for thy eternal salvation."

Look upon the saints, whose only desire is that you should join them in praising God for ever; they assure you that the path to heaven is not as difficult as the world suggests, saying, "Have courage, whoever considers the path of devotion by which we travelled here will see that it was a more delightful path than those of the world."

Election

1. I renounce hell and all its tormenting pains for ever. I renounce that eternity of misery with all its blasphemies and curses directed to God.

2. I turn myself heart and soul towards heaven with its eternal glory and unending happiness; there shall be my home for ever, in the holy mansions of eternity. O God, I bless thy mercy and choose according to thy will. O Jesus, my Saviour, I respond to thy love which has purchased for me my place in heaven, desiring nothing else but to love and bless thee for ever.

3. I accept the graces which our Lady and the saints obtain for me and promise to make my way to join their company, travelling hand in hand with my guardian angel, who will lead me there.

18. TENTH MEDITATION: CHOICE OT THE DEVOUT LIFE

Preparation

Place yourself in the presence of God and humbly ask his help.

Considerations

1. Imagine yourself again on the open plain, alone with your guardian angel, and imagine that on your left there sits the devil on a mighty throne, surrounded by his minions and countless multitudes who by their sins acknowledge him to be their lord. Look on their faces and see the rage and hatred, envy and anger written there, see how they are wasted with desire for riches, immersed in vanity, bent only on pleasures which prove empty, debased by their passions to the level of the brutes. Amongst them you will see no peace, no order and no respect, no show of love which is not mockery; such are those over whom the devil holds his cursed sway.

2. Then imagine that on your right you see Christ crucified, praying that they may escape from the devil's power and calling them to himself. See the mighty multitude of saints and angels all about him, and their beauty: men and women who in their virginity are whiter than the lily, widows full of self-denial and humility, countless married people happy in a mutual love and respect which flows from charity. See how their exterior life in no way hinders their interior life, nor their love of one another that of God.

Look upon that multitude and you will see their evident holiness and gentleness as they listen to our Lord, on whom their hopes are set. Their joy is gracious, loving and well ordered, their love for one another pure and sacred. Those in affliction are resigned and courageous, for their Saviour encourages them; all are united in their love for him.

3. So far by your resolutions you have forsaken Satan and his minions but you have yet to enlist under the

standard of Christ the King, for you are still hesitating
in your choice.

4. Our Lady and St Joseph and countless saints, who
once lived in the midst of the world, invite you and encourage you, while the crucified King calls you by name,
"Come, O my beloved one, come, that I may crown
thee."

Election

1. I will never serve under the banners of the world,
but forsake for ever its vain follies. I renounce the infer-
nal King of Pride and all his works.

2. I turn to Jesus, King of Everlasting Glory and Happiness saying: I love thee with my whole heart and unite
myself to thee with all my soul, choosing thee as my King
now and for ever, and pledge myself ever to obey thy
holy laws.

3. O Mary, my mother, I choose thee as my guide,
placing myself under thy protection and offering thee
a special love and reverence.

O my good angel, do not leave me until you have
brought me to this blessed company, with whom I will
for ever praise my chosen King.

19. GENERAL CONFESSION

HAVING made the meditations necessary for your purpose, with courage and humility and without any appre-
hension, make your confession.

Sin is shameful at the time but when repented and
confessed it serves for our salvation, while repentance
and confession are so beautiful and fragant as to banish
the ugliness and stench of sin. Simon the Leper despis-

ed Mary Magdalen as a sinner but our Lord spoke only of the greatness of her love and the perfume which she
emptied out for him. If we are truly humble, Philothea,
our sins will certainly displease us because they offend
God, yet to confess them will be a joy, because confession
honours God, while the very fact of revealing our ail-
ments to our physician is a relief in itself.

Kneel in the confessional as though on Mount Calvary at the feet of Christ crucified, whose precious blood
washes away your sins, for it is in truth that very blood
which has purchased the pardon which we obtain. Open
your whole heart that all your sins may depart and that
the graces purchased by the Passion may flow in to take
their place. Reveal everything that is on your conscience
simply and sincerely, then listen to your confessor's
advice, saying in your heart, *Speak on, Lord, thy servant
is listening*[1] for it is Christ who speaks, having said of
his priests, *He who listens to you, listens to me.*[2] Finally,
make the following solemn resolution, after having read
it carefully and meditated upon it with as much devotion as possible.

20. SOLEMN RESOLUTION

STANDING in the presence of God and before the
heavenly court and having considered his infinite mercy
and goodness to me, whom he has created, preserved,
guarded and on whom he has showered so many graces;
considering how long he has borne with my sins and
how often invited me to change my ways, waiting
patiently till this very day in spite of my ingratitude,
disloyalty and infidelity, so detrimental to me and so

[1] 1 Kings 3. 9.   [2] Luke 10. 16.

offensive to him; considering further that I became his child on the day of my baptism and that contrary to the promises then made in my name I have violated my soul and used it to sin against him so often, I at last cast myself down before his divine justice, acknowledging that I am guilty of the passion and death of Jesus Christ and deserve to be damned for ever.

My only appeal is to his infinite mercy, for which I beg while detesting with all my heart the sins of my past life; and I beg absolution for these sins in the name of my Redeemer, in whom alone I hope, and promise to renew my baptism promises, renouncing the world, the flesh and the devil from this time forward. And I firmly resolve to serve him, consecrating to him my soul with all its powers, my body with all its senses and all the desires of my heart; promising that everything in me will be used according to his will, to which I will be obedient and faithful for ever, without ever wishing to retract this pledge.

If it should happen that I yield to temptation and in any way fail in this resolution, I determine, with the help of the Holy Spirit, to turn back without delay to the Divine Mercy. I make this resolution without any reservations, in God's presence, in the sight of the Church Triumphant and in the presence of the Church Militant before whose minister I make this declaration: O eternal God, Father, Son and Holy Spirit, confirm this resolution in my heart which I offer to thee in sacrifice, and as it has pleased thee to inspire this resolution, grant me the strength and grace to carry it out. *Thou art my God, the God of my heart,*[1] the God of my soul and very being, and as such I love and adore thee now and for ever.

[1] Ps. 15. 1; 72 25.

41

21. CONCLUSION

HAVING made this solemn resolution, listen within your heart to the words of absolution pronounced by your Saviour in the sight of the angels and saints in heaven at the very moment when the priest in his name absolves you here on earth. The heavenly host rejoice at your happiness and sing for joy in seeing your heart restored to grace and holiness. What a wonderful contract you make with God, Philothea, for giving yourself to him you receive in return eternal life and God himself! All that remains is for you to take pen in hand and with a sincere heart sign your resolution; then approach the altar, where God in his turn will sign and seal your absolution and his promise of paradise by setting himself, in Communion, as a seal upon your purified heart, purging it not only from sin but even from attachment to sin.

We can never really uproot our attachments to sin as long as we live; we can, however mortify them, so I will give you some further advice which, if practised, will preserve you from yielding to them, setting before you that complete purity to which I desire to lead you.

22. PURIFICATION FROM ATTACHMENT TO VENIAL SIN

THE stronger the light, the more clearly we can see reflected in a mirror the blemishes and stains upon our face, so when the inward light of the Holy Spirit shines upon our conscience we can see more clearly the sins and imperfections on our soul while this same light arouses our desire to cleanse and purify ourselves from these hindrances to true devotion.

You will see, Philothea, that although you have been purified from mortal sin and attachment to it, your soul is still inclined and attached to venial sin.

Now to be attached and inclined to venial sin is a very different thing from actual venial sins themselves, for it is not in our power to avoid venial sins altogether for any length of time, but it is within our power to avoid being attached to them.

For example, it is one thing to tell a few lies in fun over an unimportant matter but quite another to take pleasure in lying and make a habit of it, that is why I say we must purify ourselves from all attachment to venial sin; in other words, we must never deliberately make a habit of any kind of venial sin, for to be willing to displease God is in itself displeasing to him and unworthy of us.

Since all venial sin, no matter how slight, displeases God, though not to the extent of causing him to reject us, to be attached to venial sin is to be prepared to displease God. Surely it is impossible for a generous soul to displease God and be prepared to go on doing so? Such attachment, Philothea, is as much opposed to devotion as attachment to mortal sin to charity; it weakens our spiritual powers, renders us less susceptible to divine consolation and opens the door to temptation; though it does not kill the soul it makes it very anaemic; *Ointment grows foul*, says the wise man, *when dead flies are lodged in it*[1]— in other words, flies which only touch and eat the ointment in passing do not spoil what is left but when they die in the ointment they lessen its value. In the same way venial sins cause little damage when they only touch the soul in passing but if they remain in the soul,

[1] Eccles. 10. 1.

43

because the soul is attached to them, they destroy the purity of the ointment of devotion.

Spiders do not kill bees but they spoil and corrupt their honey and spin webs about their honeycombs, preventing the bees from carrying on their work. In the same way, venial sin does not kill the soul but it spoils devotion and spins a web of bad habits and inclinations about the soul so that it is no longer able to practise charity with that zeal which we call devotion.

It is of no great importance, Philothea, to tell a small lie or to be a little careless in what we say or do, or if in our dress, our laughter, our amusements, we overdo things a little, provided that as soon as these spiritual spiders alight on our conscience we chase them off at once as the bees drive off real spiders; but if we allow them to remain in our heart and are glad to keep them there, before long we shall find the honey of our devotion wasted and the hive of our conscience entangled. However, I say again, how could it be possible for generous souls to enjoy displeasing God, be attached to what would displease him, or be ready to do anything which they know could ever offend him?

23. PURIFICATION FROM ATTACHMENT TO USELESS AND DANGEROUS THINGS

DANCES and banquets and the theatre are not evil in themselves for we can make good use of them or not, but they are nevertheless dangerous, particularly if we are attached to them, for Philothea, though there is nothing wrong in dancing or wearing fine clothes or attending the theatre, to have our hearts set upon such things hinders our devotion and herein lies the danger. I say again, such things are not wrong, but an attachment to them is wrong. Why should we fill our hearts with desires for such vain and foolish things when they only take the place of good desires or at least weaken them?

The Nazarites used to abstain, not only from everything *that may make a man drunk*, but also *from grapes and whatever was pressed out the grape*,[1] not that the grapes or their juice would make them drunk, but because it might lead them to desire to drink the wine itself. In the same way, we can make use of these dangerous things, but to set our hearts upon them would do harm to our devotion.

When stags have grown too fat they hide themselves because they know that they are out of condition and would not be able to run very fast if pursued; so if we burden our hearts with desires for useless and superfluous things we cannot run easily and freely in the ways of God, which is what we mean by devotion.

Children love to chase butterflies and no one blames their eagerness because, after all, they are only children; but it is rather pathetic and ridiculous to see those who should know better chasing eagerly after useless pleasures and in their eagerness forgetting themselves.

So, Philothea, in conclusion, we must purify ourselves from our attachments to such things which, though not in themselves contrary to devotion, yet would be so if we set our hearts upon them.

24. PURIFICATION FROM EVIL INCLINATIONS

WE have certain natural inclinations, Philothea, which are called imperfections because they give rise to various

[1] Num. 6. 3.

faults and failings which are in no way sinful; for example, St Jerome tells us that St Paula was so naturally inclined to sadness that she nearly died of sorrow when she lost her husband and her children. There was no sin here because it was not deliberate, nevertheless it was an imperfection.

Some people are naturally light-hearted, and some are too serious; some are naturally obstinate, some naturally irascible, some naturally over-affectionate; in fact there are few people in whom we may find no such imperfections. Although these things are the result of our natural temperament, we can overcome them with care and effort and in time master them entirely; in fact, Philothea, that is what we must aim at.

Just as there is no natural temperament so good that it may not be perverted by bad habits, so there is no natural temperament so difficult that it may not be overcome with care and perseverance and the grace of God. I will now advise you on the various means by which you may purify your soul from attachment to venial sin and to dangerous things, and from your imperfections, so that your conscience may be fortified more strongly than ever against mortal sin. May God give you the grace to put this advice into practice.

PART TWO

PRAYER AND THE SACRAMENTS

I. THE NECESSITY OF PRAYER

SINCE prayer opens our mind to the brightness of divine light and our will to the warmth of heavenly love, nothing so purges our mind of ignorance and our will of evil desires; its sacred waters freshes the soul, wash away our imperfections, revive the flowers of our good desires and quench the thirst of our hearts' passions.

I specially recommend mental prayer, and the prayer of the heart, in particular meditation on the life and passion of our Lord; by often looking upon him, your soul will be filled with him, you will understand the dispositions of his heart and model your actions on his. He is *The light of the world*[1] and therefore in him and by him and for him alone we must be enlightened and guided; he is the *living well of Jacob*[2] in whose waters we may cleanse ourselves.

By keeping close to him and observing what he says and does and the desires of his heart, we shall learn, with the help of his grace, to speak and act like him, just as children learn to speak by listening and chattering to their mother. Let us always remain close to him, Philothea, for it is certain that we cannot reach God the Father except through this door; as we could not see ourselves reflected in the glass of a mirror unless the back were covered with lead or tin, so we could not easily contemplate the

[1] John 8. 12   [2] John 4. 6

Divinity in this world if it were not united to the sacred humanity of Christ, whose life and death are the most appropriate, helpful and profitable subjects for our ordinary meditation. It is not for nothing that our Lord calls himself *the living bread that has come down from heaven*,[1] for as bread should be eaten with every kind of meat so our Lord should be looked upon, considered and sought after in all our prayers and actions. The various incidents of his life and death have been arranged and set out as points for meditation by various spiritual writers of whom I recommend St Bonaventure, Bellintani, Bruno, Capiglia, Granada and Da Ponte.

Spend an hour every day, some time before the midday meal, in meditation, and the earlier the better, because your mind will then be less distracted, and fresh after a night's sleep; but do not spend more than a hour unless your spiritual director expressly tells you to do so. If possible, it is best to make your meditation in church, because neither your family nor anyone else is likely to prevent you from staying there for an hour, whereas if you are dependent on others you might not be able to promise yourself an uninterrupted hour at home.

Always begin your prayers, mental or vocal, by placing yourself in the presence of God; you will soon see how helpful this is. I would advise you to say the *Pater*, *Ave* and *Credo* in Latin, while of course taking care to understand what you are saying in your own language so that while using the language of the Church you may lose nothing of the sacred meaning of these wonderful prayers. Be very careful to attend to what you are saying and conform your heart to the sentiments expressed. Do

[1] John 6. 51

48

not try to say too many prayers but say with sincerity those that you do say; one *Pater* said devoutly being of greater value than many said hastily.

The Rosary is a very helpful form of prayer, provided you know how to use it properly; if you do not know, there are many booklets which will teach you. It is also good to say the litanies of our Lord of our Lady, and of the saints and any of the prayers printed in approved prayer books, but remember that if you are able to make mental prayer you should always put that first. Don't be anxious if you then find that for any reason you must omit vocal prayers, but be content with saying (either before or after your meditation) the *Pater*, *Ave* and *Credo*. If during vocal prayer you feel drawn to interior or mental prayer do not resist this interior attraction; allow your mind to turn gently in that direction and do not worry because you have not said as many vocal prayers as you intended, the mental prayer which has taken their place being much more pleasing to God and much more profitable to your soul. One exception to this rule, of course, is the Divine Office if we are bound to say it, for in that case we must first fulfil our obligation.

If, because you are very busy, or for any other reason you miss your morning prayer, try to make up for this loss after the midday meal, as long after it as possible, because if you try to pray while you are still digesting your food you will only feel drowsy and it might harm your health.

If you cannot find any time for mental prayer during the day, make up for it by saying many ejaculatory prayers, by spiritual reading or some act of penance to correct your failure, making a firm resolution not to miss your prayer tomorrow.

2. THE PRESENCE OF GOD

As you may not know how to practise mental prayer, Philothea, for unfortunately it is a lost art in our age, I will give you a simple method which will help you until, by reading some of the useful books on the subject, and above all by the practice itself, you are more fully instructed. The first thing is to place yourself in the presence of God and ask his help, so I will begin by showing you four ways of placing yourself in his presence.

The first way is to realize more vividly the omnipresence of God, in other words, the fact that God is everywhere and in everything, that nowhere and in nothing in this world may he not be found. Just as the birds, wherever they fly, always encounter the air, so we, wherever we go or wherever we are, find God present. Everyone knows this but few give it much thought.

Blind men, when told that they are in the presence of a prince, behave with respect, even though they cannot see him, yet for that very reason they forget his presence and so more easily lose their respect and reverence. Our trouble is, Philothea, that though we know by our faith that God is present, we do not see him with our eyes and so we often forget and behave as though he were not there. To know that God is present everywhere and never to think about it, comes to the same thing as if we did not know at all.

Before prayer, then, we must awaken our realization of God's presence as David did when he said: *If I should climb up to heaven, thou art there, if I sink down to the world beneath, thou art present still,*[1] or make use of the

[1] Ps. 138. 8.

words of Jacob when he saw the ladder: *How terrible is
this place; indeed the Lord is in this place and I knew it not.*[1]

When Jacob says that he *knew it not,* he means that he
was not thinking of it at the time; for he could not have
been ignorant of the fact that God is everywhere. When
you begin our prayer, then, say from the bottom of your
heart: "God is truly here".

The second way of placing yourself in God's presence is
to realize that he is not only present in the place where you
are, but also in a very special way, in the depths of your
soul, which he enlightens and sanctifies by his presence,
since he is, as it were, the heart of your heart, the soul of
your soul. Just as the soul is present in every part of the
body and yet resides in a special way in the heart, so God,
though present everywhere, is present in a special way
in the soul and that is why David called him *the God of
his heart*[2] and why St Paul says: *in him we lived and move
and have our being.*[3] By considering this truth you will
awaken in your heart a great reverence for God, who is so
intimately present there.

The third way is to think of our Lord in his sacred
humanity, seeing everyone from heaven, gazing particularly upon Christians and more especially upon Christians
at prayer.

This is no mere imagination but a most certain truth, for
though we cannot see him, he certainly looks down upon
us, as was revealed to St Stephen at the time of his martyrdom. So we can truly say: *he is standing on the other
side of this very wall. . . looking in through each window
in turn, peering through every chink.*[4]

The fourth way is to use our imagination to represent
our Lord as very near to us in the same way as we often

[1] Gen. 28. 17.   [2] Ps. 72. 26   [3] Acts 17. 28   [4] Cant 2. 9

think of our friends when we say, "I imagine I can see such and such a person doing this or that", or when we say, "It seems to me that he is really here"; but if we are praying in the presence of the Blessed Sacrament, then this presence will be real and not merely imaginary for our Lord is really present under the appearance of the bread which is, as it were, a veil through which he sees and watches us, though we cannot see him with our eyes.

To place yourself in the presence of God before prayer, choose one of these four ways, never more than one, and then dwell upon it only briefly and simply.

3. ASKING GOD'S HELP

Once you have realized you are in the presence of God, cast yourself down with deep reverence before him and acknowledge your unworthiness to appear in his majestic presence, asking for all the graces you need to serve him well, knowing that in his goodness he longs to grant them to you.

If you like, you can use some of the invocations from the psalms, such as *Do not banish me from thy presence, O God; do not take thy holy spirit away from me.*[1] *Smile on thy servant once more and I will contemplate the wonders of thy law.*[2] *Enlighten me, to scan thy law closely, and keep true to it with all my heart.*[3] *Perfect in thy own servant's heart the knowledge of thy will.*[4]

It is a very good thing to invoke your guardian angel and the holy persons concerned in the mystery you are considering; for example if it is the death of Chirst, invoke Mary, St John, Mary Magdalen and the Good Thief, so

[1] Ps. 50. 13.   [2] Ps. 30. 17; 118. 18.   [3] Ps. 118. 34
[4] Ps. 118. 125.

that they may obtain for you the interior graces which they were granted at the time; or if you are meditating on your own death, ask your guardian angel, who will be with you then, to inspire you with suitable considerations, and so on for the rest.

4. FURTHER PREPARATION

AFTER you have placed yourself in God's presence and asked his help, in some meditations it is useful to represent to the imagination the scene of the mystery you are considering as if it were actually taking place before you; for example, if you wish to meditate on the Crucifixion imagine yourself on Mount Calvary and that you see and hear all that took place on the day of the Passion; or if you like, for it comes to the same thing, imagine that the Crucifixion is taking place in the very place where you are, just as the Evangelists describe it.

The same applies to meditations on death or hell and to all similar mysteries concerned with things that we can see and hear and touch, for with regard to other mysteries such as the greatness of God, the beauty of virtue, the reason for our creation, and so on, we cannot possibly use our imagination, though it is true that we may make use of some comparison or analogy to help us to consider such invisible things. However, I do not wish to make prayer seem too difficult or wearying but rather as simple as possible. To imagine the scene is to keep our mind on the mystery we are considering so that it may not wander to and fro, just as we confine a bird in its cage or a hawk to our wrist.

Some will tell you that it is better to represent these mysteries to yourself in an entirely intellectual and spiritual way, through faith, or else consider that the events take place within your own soul, but this is rather too subtle to begin with; so Philothea, until God raises you higher, remain in the valley which I have pointed out to you.

5. CONSIDERATIONS

AFTER using your imagination you begin to use your understanding, and this is what we call meditation; in other words, making use of considerations to raise your heart to God and to the things of God. This is where meditation differs from study and from considerations which are made to become learned, or to write or to engage in discussion.

Having confined your spirit, as I have said, within the mystery you are considering, either by using your imagination, if it is something perceptible to the senses, or by the mind itself if it is something invisible, begin to consider, in the way explained in the meditations which I have already given you. As long as you are gaining light and help from any one consideration stay there without passing on, as the bees do, who never leave a flower so long as they can still find some honey there; but if you find a consideration unhelpful after having tried it for a while, pass on to another, but proceed very gently and simply in this matter without any undue haste.

6. SPIRITUAL ACTS AND RESOLUTIONS

MEDITATION moves our will to make spiritual acts such as the love of God and our neighbour, desire of heaven and eternal glory, or zeal for the salvation of souls; it makes us long to be like our Lord, awakens a sense of compassion, wonder and joy, or fear of offending God or of judgement and hell; it leads us to hate sin and have confidence in the goodness and mercy of God and to be ashamed of the sins of our past life.

We should make these spiritual acts as whole-heartedly as possible. However, Philothea, you must not dwell upon them to such an extent that you forget to make practical resolutions according to your own special needs; for example, the first words of our Lord on the Cross will surely arouse in your soul a desire to forgive your enemies and to love them, but this is of little value unless it leads you to make a special resolution to that end, saying to yourself, "I resolve not to be annoyed any more by anything which so and so—perhaps a neighbour or a servant—may say to me, nor by any affront which some other person may offer me; on the contrary, I will say this or that to win him over", and so on. In this way, Philothea, you will correct your faults in a very short time; but if you rely upon your spiritual acts alone it will take you a very long time and be very difficult.

7. CONCLUSION OF PRAYER

MEDITATION should be brought to a close by three spiritual acts, made with as much humility as possible.

The first, an act of thanksgiving to God for the spiritual acts and resolutions which he has inspired in us and for his goodness and mercy which our meditation has revealed anew to us; the second an oblation to God of our desires and resolutions, in union with the passion and death of his Son, his virtues, his goodness and his mercy;

the third, an act of petition to our Father for the graces and virtues of his Son, for a blessing on our resolutions that we may put them into practice faithfully, praying further for the Church, for priests and for our relatives and friends; then ask our Lady, the angels and the saints to intercede for us, concluding with a *Pater* and *Ave*, the general and necessary prayers for all the faithful.

I have suggested that after all this one should gather a bouquet of devotion and what I mean is this: those who walk in a lovely garden are loth to leave it without taking away a few flowers to keep with them during the day, whose fragrance will give them pleasure. In the same way, having meditated on some mystery, we should choose a few thoughts which we found helpful and useful to our spiritual progress, so that we may call them to mind during the day and spiritually breathe their fragrance. It is as well to gather this bouquet of spiritual thoughts while still where we made our meditation, or while walking about alone for a short time afterwards.

8. FURTHER ADVICE ON MEDITATION

ABOVE all, Philothea, after your meditation, remember your resolutions so that you may carefully put them into practice during the day.

Such resolutions are the fruit of meditation, which would be useless without them, or even harmful, since to meditate on virtues which we do not practise sometimes makes us proud, considering ourselves to be in fact what we have only resolved to be; which doubtless we should be, if our resolutions were strong and well founded; but if unpractised they are as certainly useless and dangerous.

We must, then, do all we can to put them into practice, making use of every available opportunity, great or small. For example, if I have made up my mind to win over by gentleness someone who has offended me, I shall seek an opportunity of meeting him that day so that I may greet him amicably. If this should fail, at least I shall try to speak well of him and pray for him to God.

When you have finished your meditation, take care to keep your heart undisturbed lest you spill the balm it has received; in other words, keep silence as long as possible and transfer your attention to other things quietly, trying to retain the fruits of your prayer as long as you can. A man who carries a vessel full of some precious liquid walks very carefully, looking neither right nor left but straight ahead to avoid stumbling over a stone or making a false step, making sure that the vessel is well balanced. This is how you must act after prayer, trying not to be too quickly distracted; for example, should you meet someone you must speak to, accept this as unavoidable, but keep a guard on your heart, so that you spill as little of the balm of prayer as possible. You must learn how to pass from prayer to the duties of your state, no matter how far removed they seem from the thoughts you had in your prayer. The lawyer must learn to pass from prayer to pleading a cause; the business man to commerce, the married woman to her housework, with such gentleness and tranquillity that the soul is not disturbed. Since both prayer and the duties of our state are God's will, we should pass from one to the other with humility and devotion.

It may happen that you find your heart raised up to God from the very beginning of your prayer, in which case there is no need to follow the method I have suggested, for though considerations usually come first, if the Holy Spirit has already brought this about they would be to no purpose. We should always follow the movements of our heart whenever they come, before or after our considerations, which I have placed first only as the general rule, and the same follows with regard to our thanksgiving, offering and petitions, all of which may spring from our considerations. These spiritual acts must not be restrained, any more than the other affections, though we should repeat them when we bring our meditation to an end. However, with regard to our resolutions, we should make these last of all; relating as they do to more personal and familiar things, they might otherwise distract us.

While making our spiritual acts and resolutions, it is useful to address ourselves sometimes to our Lord, sometimes to the angels or to the persons represented in the mysteries to the saints, to sinners, to ourselves or, even, as David in the Psalms, and other saints in their prayers and meditations, to inanimate creatures.

9. DRYNESS IN PRAYER

IF it happens, Philothea, that you find neither satisfaction nor consolation in your prayer, do not be in the least worried, but say some vocal prayers, tell our Lord about it and admit how unworthy you are; ask him to help you, kiss the crucifix, saying with Jacob, *I will not let thee go, except thou bless me,*[1] or, with the woman of Canaan, *even the dogs feed on the crumbs that fall from their master's table.*[2]

At other times read some spiritual book quietly until your soul is more disposed to prayer. Stir up your heart by

[1] Gen. 32. 26.   [2] Matt. 15. 27.

outward acts of devotion, such as prostrating yourself on the ground, crossing your hands upon your breast or embracing the crucifix, provided of course you are in some private place. If, after all this, you still find no consolation, remain untroubled, however spiritually dry you may feel; just remain devoutly in God's presence; think how many courtiers go into the presence of the prince hundreds of times without any hope of speaking to him but only to be seen by him and to pay their respects. In the same way, Philothea, we come to prayer, purely and simply to pay our respects to God and prove our loyalty. If it pleases him to speak to us by granting us his inspirations and interior consolations, that would be a great honour and delight, but if he does not show us such favour and leaves us there unnoticed without so much as speaking to us, we must leave on that account but on the contrary remain quietly and devoutly in his presence. There can be no doubt that our patience will please him; he will notice our diligence and perseverance and favour us another time with his consolations and let us realize the sweetness of prayer, but even if this should be denied us, let us be satisfied, Philothea, that it is honour enough for us just to be near him and in his presence.

10. MORNING PRAYER

As well as daily mental and vocal prayer, there are other shorter prayers which are, as it were, offshoots of your main prayer; to begin with, that which you make first thing in the morning to prepare for all you are going to do that day.

You may make it as follows:

1. Thank God most lovingly for keeping you alive

until this morning, and if during the past night you fell into any sin ask his forgiveness.

2. Consider that this day is given you to win the day of eternity and resolve to make good use of it to that end.

3. Anticipate the various opportunities you will have during the day to serve God, as well as the temptations you may encounter, for example, temptations to anger, vanity, lack of restraint and so on. Then resolve (*a*) to make good use of the opportunities to advance in the love of God and (*b*) to resist and avoid anything contrary to the good of your soul and God's glory, determining also how you will put this into practice. For example, if you anticipate a discussion with some hot-tempered person, resolve not to offend him but also choose beforehand what you will say, avoiding any words which might annoy him, or arrange for someone else to be present to ensure that he keeps his temper. If you anticipate a visit to a sick person, resolve on the time of your visit, the particular help you will give him and so on.

4. Having humbled yourself before God, assured that without him you can keep none of these resolutions either to avoid evil or to do good, take your heart, as it were in your hands and offer it to him full of your good intentions, begging him to take care of it and strengthen it to serve him well. You may use the following or similar words: "Behold, O Lord, my poor heart which through your goodness has conceived many good desires but is too weak and wretched to put them into practice unless you grant your heavenly grace. This I beg, O merciful Father, through the passion of thy Son to whose honour I consecrate this and all my days."

Invoke our Lady, your guardian angel and the saints, that they may help you.

All this should be done briefly and fervently, if possible before leaving your room, so that all your actions during the day may be watered by God's blessing. Never, Philothea, I beg of you, omit this morning prayer.

II. EVENING PRAYER

As before the midday meal you should nourish your soul by means of meditation, so before your evening meal you should do the same, setting aside some time alone to kneel before God in the presence of Christ Crucified, gazing on him with the eyes of your soul. Stir up again in your heart the fire of your morning meditation by many acts of love and humility towards your Saviour by recalling those points which helped you most, or by considering some new subject, whichever you prefer. Before you pray, you should examine your conscience in the usual way as follows:

1. Thank God for having preserved you during the day.

2. Examine your behaviour in the course of it, and this is done easily of you remember where you have been, with whom and what you have been doing.

3. If you find that you have done any good, thank God; if on the other hand you find that you have done anything wrong in thought or in deed, ask his pardon, resolve to make amends for it and to confess it at the next opportunity.

4. Lastly commend your body and soul, the Church and your relatives and friends to the care of his Divine Providence. Ask our Lady, your guardian angel and the saints to watch over you and take care of you; and so with his blessing take that rest which is necessary for you according to his will.

As in the case of your morning prayer this must not be forgotten, remembering that as by your morning prayer you open the windows of your soul to the sun of justice, so by your evening prayer you close them against the shades of the night.

12. SPIRITUAL RECOLLECTION

I WISH you to pay particular attention to this point, Philothea, for it is a certain means of your spiritual advancement. Remember God's presence as often as you can during the day, using any of the ways I have mentioned. Remember what he is doing and what you are doing; seeing his eyes upon you filled with incomparable love, say: "O God, why do I not always look on you as you are always looking on me? Why, when you think so often of me, do I think so seldom of you? O my soul, my true place is in God, and where do I so often find myself?"

As the birds have nests in the trees to which they may fly for rest, and as the deer have their bushes and thickets in which to hide and shelter themselves and enjoy the coolness of the shade in summer, so, Philothea, our hearts should seek out some place every day either on Mount Calvary or in the wounds of our Lord or in some other place near him, to which we may retire occasionally for rest and peace and forget our exterior occupations, and defend ourselves against temptation as in a castle.

What joy if we can say sincerely to our Lord: *Thou art my stronghold of defence. to save me from peril,* [1] *my shade from the day's heat, my refuge to give me shelter from storm and rain.* [2]

Remember to retire often then, Philothea, into the so-

[1] Ps. 30. 3.   [2] Cf. Isa. 4. 6.

litude of your heart while you are outwardly engaged in
work or with others. This spiritual solitude can be preserved no matter how many people there are about you,
for they are only about your body and not about your
heart, which can remain all alone with God. This is what
David practised in the midst of his various occupations,
as he says so often in his Psalms: *O Lord, I am ever close
to thee.*[1] *Always I can keep the Lord within sight.*[2] *Unto
thee I lift up my eyes, unto thee, who dwellest in the
thee I lift up my eyes, unto thee, who dwellest in the hea-
vens.*[3] *On the Lord I fix my eyes continually.*[4]

In any case our work is rarely so serious that we cannot now and then stand aside from it and enter this place
of divine solitude. When St Catherine of Siena's parents
deprived her of the time and place for prayer and meditation, our Lord inspired her to make her soul a shrine
to which she could retire with him in spirit in the midst
of her exterior occupations. Worldly criticism caused her
no inconvenience for the same reason; she merely shut
herself in this interior shrine, she said, and found consolation with her heavenly spouse. After this she always
advised her followers to make a shrine of their own hearts
in which to dwell.

Often withdraw, then, in spirit into this shrine, where,
alone, you may speak heart to heart with God, saying
with David: *I keep watch; I am no better than a pelican out
in the desert, an owl on some ruined dwelling; lonely as a
single sparrow on the house top.*[5]

Literally these words indicate that this great king spent
hours alone contemplating spiritual things, while in their
mystical sense they indicate three ways of imitating the

[1] Ps. 72.23. [2] Ps. 15. 8. [3] Ps. 122. 1.
[4] Ps. 24. 15. [5] Ps. 101.7, 8.

solitude of our Lord, who on Mount Calvary was like a pelican in the desert feeding her young with her own blood; who at his birth in a deserted stable was like an owl in a ruined house, mourning and weeping over our imperfections and our sins; and who on the day of his Ascension was like a sparrow flying upwards towards heaven, as to the house-top of the world. To these three places then, we can retire in spirit amid the tumult of our exterior occupations.

When Blessed Elzear, Count of Arian in Provence, had been long away from Delphina, his devout and chaste wife, she sent a messenger to ask how he was; he answered, "My dear wife, I am very well; but if you desire to see me, seek me in the wound in the side of Jesus, for that is where I dwell; there you will find me. Seek elsewhere and you will seek in vain." He was truly a Christian knight.

13. ASPIRATIONS AND GOOD THOUGHTS

WE retire to God because we aspire to him and we aspire to him to retire to him, these two things mutually supporting each other while both spring from good thoughts. Make frequent, ardent, heartfelt aspirations to God, Philothea; wonder at his beauty, ask his help, cast yourself in spirit at the foot of the Cross, adore his goodness, often speak to him about your salvation, offer him your heart a hundred times a day, gaze with the eyes of your soul upon his gentleness and take his hand so that he may guide you; place him as a fragrant bouquet on your breast and as a standard in your heart.

In other words, by countless movements of your heart give yourself to your divine Spouse, stirring up a passionate and tender love for him. Such is the kind of prayer recommended by St Augustine to the devout Proba. By such intimate intercourse with God, Philothea, your soul will become filled with the perfumes of his perfection, and after all it is not so difficult, for it can be fitted into your daily occupations and work, without in any way hindering them. It only involves turning aside for a short time, and helps rather than hinders us, as a pilgrim who halts for a while to refresh himself with a little wine does not hinder his journey but rather gains fresh strength to speed him on his way, taking rest only to go forward more swiftly.

There are many collections of short vocal prayers which may be useful, but if you take my advice you will not restrict yourself to any set form of words; rather say aloud or in your heart whatever love suggests to you at the time, for it will inspire you with all you desire. It is true that certain words are especially satisfying to the heart, such as the aspirations found so abundantly in the various invocations of the name of Jesus, or the expressions of love in the Canticle of Canticles; hymns are also very useful, so long as they are sung devoutly. The thoughts of men in love, with a merely natural love, are always turned towards their beloved, their hearts full of love for her, her praises always on their lips; when absent they constantly express their love in letters; they carve her name on every tree; so those who love God never stop thinking of him, longing for him, seeking him and speaking to him; if it were possible they would engrave the sacred name of Jesus on the breast of everyone in the world. Every created thing serves their love and speaks the praise of their beloved. St Augustine, quoting St Antony, says that everything in the world speaks to them silently yet clearly of their love; everything inspires good thoughts which lift their hearts to God.

Here are some examples:

St Gregory Nazianzen, once walking on the sea shore noticed how the waves as they crept over the sand left behind them many little shells, bits of seaweed and rubbish cast up by the sea, while other waves swept them back yet, no matter how violent, left the rocks nearby unmoved. Reflecting on this, he considered that those who are weak, like the shells and bits of seaweed, allow themselves to be swept to and fro by the joys and troubles of life on the crest of the waves of fortune, while the courageous remain steadfast as rocks no matter how strong the storm. This thought led him to say with David, *O God, save me; see how the waters close about me, theatening my very life! Save me from sinking in the mire, rescue me from my enemies, from the deep waters that surround me.*[1] For this happened when the usurpation of his see by Maximus was causing him great anxiety.

St Fulgentius, Bishop of Ruspe, was present at a gathering of Roman nobles when Theodoric, King of the Goths, was making a speech; noticing the splendour of those present drawn up according to their rank, he said in his heart: "O God, how beautiful the heavenly Jerusalem must be when the earthly Rome appears so glorious. If in this world such splendour is granted to those who seek vanity, what glory must await, in the world to come, those who seek truth."

St Anselm, Archbishop of Canterbury, is said to have been admirable in this practice of good thoughts. Once when he was on a journey, a hare, fleeing from the hounds and in danger of death, sought refuge between the

[1] Ps. 68. 2, 15.

feet of his horse; the baying hounds did not dare to violate the sanctuary of their prey. The hunters were amused but Anselm wept and sighed, saying, "You may laugh, but this poor animal does not. So the soul, harassed and pursued by its enemies, hounded by every kind of temptation, pursued to the very gates of death, seeks fearfully for a place of refuge and safety, mocked and laughed at if it cannot find it." And having said this he went on his way sorrowful.

The fact that Constantine the Great had written with great respect to St Antony having greatly astonished his monks, he said to them, "Why are you so astonished that a king should write to a man? It is more astonishing that God should write his law for mortal men, and that he has spoken to them face to face in the person of his Son."

St Francis, noticing a single sheep in a flock of goats, said to his companion, "See how gentle this poor sheep is among the goats; so was our Lord gentle and humble among the Pharisees." On another occasion he saw a lamb being devoured by a hog and said weeping, "O how clearly the death of this lamb pictures the death of our Lord". When our great contemporary, Francis Borgia, was Duke of Gandia he used to make many devout reflections when out hawking. "I used to marvel", he said later, "at the fact that falcons return to the fist and allow themselves to be hooded and chained while men are so slow to obey the laws of God." St Basil used to say that the rose among the thorns utters this warning: "The pleasures of the world, O mortal men, are ringed about with sadness. Nothing in the world is pure. There is no joy without regret, no marriage without widowhood, no harvest without labour, no glory without humiliation, no honour which is not paid for, no delight without weariness or health without sickness. The rose's loveliness speaks of sorrow for it speaks of sin which condemned the earth to bring forth thorns."

A devout person gazing on a stream on a still night and seeing reflected on its surface heaven and all its stars said: "My God, when thou hast brought me to heaven these very stars will be beneath my feet; and as these stars are reflected here below, so men on earth are reflected in the living waters of thy love." Another person watching a river flow by said, "My soul will never be at rest until it flows into the infinite sea which is its source." St Frances used to pray upon the bank of a little stream and once in an ecstasy she repeated softly these words: "The grace of my God flows gently like the waters of this stream." Another seeing the trees in blossom sighed and said: "Why am I alone without blossom in the garden of the Church?"; and another, seeing some chickens beneath their mother's wing, said: *O God, hide me under the shelter of thy wings.*[1] Yet another, looking at a sunflower, said: "When, O God, will my soul open out under the warmth of thy love?" and the same person seeing some pansies, beautiful but without fragrance said: "My thoughts are like that; beautiful but of no effect."

So, Philothea, you will see how everything about us in this world inspires good thoughts and desires; how unhappy are those who turn created things away from God and make them serve sin; but how happy those who turn all things to the glory of their Creator, and make them serve the truth. St Gregory Nazianzen used to say, "It is my practice to make all things serve my spiritual good." If you read the words of St Jerome concerning St Paula you will see how often he refers to the good thoughts and

[1] Ps. 16. 8.

desires she used to draw from everything that happened to her. This practice of spiritual retirement and ejaculatory prayer is at the very heart of devotion, and though it can make up for the lack of other prayers, nothing can take its place; without it we cannot lead the contemplative or the active life properly. Without it relaxation is only idleness and work a distraction; so, I beg you, never fail to practise it with all your heart.

14. ATTENDING MASS

So far I have not mentioned the most important and sacred of all devotions, namely the sacrifice and sacrament of the Mass. The Mass lies at the very heart of the Christian religion and devotion, a most wonderful mystery, containing within itself the fountainhead of love, and is the chief means used by God in pouring out upon us his graces and favours. Prayer when united to this divine sacrifice has unspeakable power, filling the soul with the blessing of heaven. In this way *leaning upon the arm of her true love*,[1] the soul *makes her way, erect as a column of smoke, all myrrh and incense, and those sweet scents the perfumer knows*.[2] Do all you can to attend Mass every day so that with the priest you may offer the sacrifice of your Redeemer to God the Father for yourself and the whole Church. St John Chrysostom says that countless angels always attend to honour this sacred mystery; in such company and for the same end, we cannot help receiving many graces. It is here that the choirs of the Church Triumphant and the Church Militant meet and are united with our Lord, so that with him, in him and

[1] Cant. 8. 5.   [2] Cant. 3. 6.

69

through him, they may captivate the heart of God the Father and obtain his mercy. What happiness to contribute by our own devotion to so precious and desirable a good! If you find it impossible to go to Mass, at least visit the church in spirit some time during the morning and unite your intention with that of all Christians, making the same spiritual acts as if you were really present at Mass in that church.

To attend Mass properly, either actually or spiritually, make your preparation with the priest from the beginning until he goes up to the altar, by putting yourself in the presence of God, acknowledging your unworthiness and asking pardon for your sins. From then until he begins reading the Gospel, consider quite simply and in a general way the birth and life of our Lord. From the Gospel to the end of the *Credo* consider his preaching and resolve to live and die faithful to his word, as a member of the Church. From the *Credo* to the *Paternoster* consider his passion and death actually symbolized by the sacrifice which, with the priest and the rest of the congregation, you offer to God the Father for his honour and your salvation. From the *Paternoster* to the Communion stir up countless desires in your heart, longing to be united to your Saviour in eternal love. From the Communion to the end thank our Lord for his Incarnation, his life, his death and for the love he manifests in the Eucharist, begging him to be always merciful to you, your relatives and friends and to the whole Church. Then with heartfelt humility and devotion receive the divine blessing which our Lord gives you through his priest. If you would rather meditate on the mystery you are considering that day, there in no need to set it aside to hear Mass as I have suggested; it will be quite sufficient if, at the beginning of Mass, you make the intention of offering the sacrifice in that way because in every meditation the acts I have suggested are included, either implicitly or explicitly.

15. OTHER PUBLIC DEVOTIONS

BESIDES hearing Mass, Philothea, try whenever you can to go to Vespers on Sundays and holy days of obligatiion for we should try to honour God more on those days especially dedicated to him. By doing this you will experience great consolation, like St Augustine, who says in his *Confessions*, that when attending Divine Office at the beginning of his conversion, his heart was filled with tenderness and his eyes with tears of devotion. It is certain that the public devotions of the Church are much more profitable and consoling than those which we choose ourselves, God having ordained that devotions in common should always be preferred to private ones. Be ready to join your local confraternities, especially those whose exercises are most fruitful and edifying. To do this is to practise a kind of obedience most pleasing to God, for though we are not commanded to join any confraternity, the Church recommends it and grants indulgences and privileges to those who join to encourage as many as possible. Further, to co-operate with others in their good works is to practise charity and though you may do just as much good by yourself as you would in a confraternity and perhaps enjoy it more, nevertheless to work with others gives greater glory to God. This applies to all public prayers and devotions in which we should take part as far as possible, edifying those about us by our good example, desiring the glory of God and praying for everyone's intentions.

16. THE INVOCATION OF THE SAINTS

As God often sends us inspirations by his angels, we should often send him our aspirations through them. The souls who live in heaven with the angels, and whom our Lord says are *as the angels*,[1] share their work by inspiring us and interceding for us. Let us unite our hearts to theirs, Philothea, learning, like young nightingales in the company of older ones, how to sing the divine praises more perfectly, saying with David, *I will sing of thy praise, angels for my witness.*[2]

Honour, reverence, and respect the blessed Virgin Mary with special love, for as the mother of Jesus Christ who is our brother, she is truly our mother. Fly to her as a little child, cast yourself upon her breast with complete confidence; invoke her motherly love and try to imitate her virtues with filial love. Make friends with the angels, who though invisible are always with you; have a special love and reverence for the angel of your diocese, for the guardian angels of those about you but most of all for your own. Often invoke them, constantly praise them, and make good use of their help and assistance in all your spiritual and temporal affairs, working together for the same intentions. Pierre Lefèvre,[3] returning one day from Germany where he had done great work for the glory of God and passing through the diocese in which he was born, said that while travelling among heretics he had received countless blessings by invoking the guardian angel of the parishes he came to, that he had been conscious of their help by the fact that they had protected him from being ambushed and had softened and prepared the hearts of

[1] Matt. 22. 30.   [2] Ps. 137.1
[3] The first priest, the first teacher and the first professor of Theology of the Society of Jesus, also the first companion of its founder St Ignatius.

many to accept his preaching. He was so emphatic about this that a young lady who heard him could repeat his words more than sixty years later.

Choose some particular saints whose lives you can best appreciate and imitate and in whose intercession you have particular confidence. The saint whose name you bear has already been assigned to you at you baptism.

17. HEARING AND READING THE WORD OF GOD

HAVE great devotion to the word of God, listening to it attentively and reverently, whether in private conversations with your friends or in sermons. Try to benefit from it, not allowing it to fall to the ground but catching it in your heart as a precious balm; like our Lady, who kept all that was said in praise of her Child most carefully in her heart. Remember that our Lord remembers all we say to him in prayer in the measure in which we remember all he says to us in preaching.

Always keep by you some good book of devotion, for example, by St Bonaventure, Gerson, Denis the Carthusian, Louis Blosius, Granada, Stella, Arias, Pinelli, Da Ponte, Avila, or the *Spiritual Combat*, the *Confessions* of St Augustine, the letters of St Jerome and so on; and read a little every day as though it were a letter from the saints in heaven to guide and encourage you on your way there.

Read also the biographies and lives of the saints in which you will see the Christian life reflected as in a mirror, benefiting from their example according to your own state in life; for although those who live in the world cannot imitate everything the saints have done, they can imitate some things, for example the solitude of St Paul, the first hermit, by making a retreat; the complete poverty of St Francis by spiritual poverty and so on. Some biographies throw light on our own lives, like those of St Teresa, St Charles Borromeo, St Bernard or the Chronicles of St Francis, while in others there is more to admire than to imitate, as in the case of St Mary of Egypt, St Simon Stylites, St Catherine of Siena or St Catherine of Genoa, but nevertheless they can at least awaken in us a desire for the love of God.

18. INSPIRATIONS

By inspirations we mean all those interior attractions, movements of the heart, pangs of conscience, and illuminations of the mind by which God, in his fatherly love and care, prevents our hearts with his blessings, to awaken, stir, urge, and attract us to virtue, charity and good resolutions, in fact to everthing that serves our eternal good. This is what is meant in the Canticle of Canticles by the beloved knocking at the door, speaking to the heart of his spouse, awaking her when she sleeps, calling for her when she is absent, inviting her to eat his honey and gather apples and flowers in his garden, to sing and let her sweet voice sound in his ears.[1]

When a man wishes to marry, three things are necessary; first he must propose, secondly the lady he wishes to marry must consider his proposal, and thirdly, she must consent. God acts in this way when he wishes to do, in, through and with us, some act of charity. First he proposes to us by his inspiration, secondly we consider it, and thirdly we consent. Just as there are there downward steps to vice—temptation, pleasure, and consent—

---

[1] Cf. Cant. 5. 1, 2; 2. 10, 13, 14; 6. 1. Isa. 40. 40. 2. Osee.2. 14.

so there are three corresponding steps upward to virtue: the inspiration, which corresponds to the temptation, pleasure in the inspiration corresponding to the pleasure in the temptation, and consent to the inspiration corresponding to the consent to the temptation.

The inspiration itself, though it last a lifetime, would not make us pleasing to God if we took no pleasure in it; on the contrary, we would offend him as did the Israelites, whom he urged to conversion for forty years and who all that time would not listen, so that he *took an oath in anger: They shall never attain my rest.*[1] In the same way, a man would be offended if he had courted a lady for a long time and she refused even to consider his proposal.

To take pleasure in inspirations disposes us to give glory to God and pleases him, for though it is not the same as consent it leads to it. As it is good and healthy sign if we take pleasure in listening to the word of God, so it is a good thing and pleasing to God if we take delight in his interior inspirations; referring to this pleasure the sacred spouse says, *How my heart melted at the sound of his voice.*[2]

So a suitor is already grateful and counts himself favoured when he sees that his attentions please his beloved. In the last analysis it is consent which perfects an act of virtue; if we withhold consent after receiving and taking pleasure in the inspiration we show ourselves ungrateful, displeasing God by despising his favours, as happened to the spouse in the Canticle; for though her heart was touched and made joyful at the voice of her beloved, she made some frivolous excuse and left him at the door, with the result that, rightly displeased, he left her and went his way.

[1] Ps. 94. 11. [2] Cant. 5. 6.

A suitor whose attentions had long been favourably received is rightly more upset if in the end they are repulsed than if they had never been considered in the first place. Resolve, then Philothea, to accept all God's inspirations whole-heartedly, receiving them as ambassadors from the King of Heaven, proposing marriage. Listen quietly to their proposals, considering the love which inspired them, cherishing and consenting to every inspiration completely, lovingly and steadfastly. If you do this, though he cannot be under any obligation to you, God will, as it were, hold himself bound by your love. Before you consent to inspirations concerning important or extraordinary matters, seek the advice of your confessor, that he may examine whether they are true or false and so preserve you from deception; for the devil often sends false inspirations to deceive those who receive them readily, but he can never deceive those who humbly obey their confessor. Once you have given consent to an inspiration, seek to put it into practice diligently; this is the height of virtue, for to consent to an inspiration in your heart without putting it into practice would be like planting a vine without desiring it to be fruitful. Morning prayer and spiritual retirement are most helpful in this matter, for they dispose us to do good not only in general but in individual circumstances.

19. CONFESSION

OUR Lord has left the sacrament of penance to his Church that we may be cleansed from the defilement of our sins as often as we fall.

Never allow your heart to remain long in a state of sin, Philothea, when such a simple remedy lies to hand.

As a lioness defiled by a leopard hastens to cleanse herself before the return of her mate lest the stench offend
and provoke him, so, if we have yielded to sin, should
we hasten in horror to cleanse ourselves as soon as possible out of respect; for God's eyes are upon us. Why should
we die spiritually when so perfect a remedy is available?
Go to confession every week, humbly and devoutly, and
always, if possible, before going to Communion, even
though you may not have any mortal sins on your conscience, for confession not only absolves venial sins but
also strengthens you to avoid falling into the same sins
again, enlightens you to recognize them more clearly and
repairs the damage they may have caused. You will be
practising humility, obedience, simplicity and charity, in
fact more virtues than in any other single act.

Be sincerely sorry for the sins you confess, however
slight, firmly resolving to avoid them in future. Those
who make a habit of confessing their venial sins without thought of amendment remain under the weight
of them all their life to the detriment of their spiritual
advancement. If you confess a lie which harmed no one,
that you have said something out of place or given too
much time to amusements, be genuinely sorry and
make a firm promise of amendment, for it is an abuse to
confess any kind of sin, mortal or venial, unless you will
to be freed from it, for that is the very purpose of confession. Avoid vague accusations such as "I have not loved God as much as I ought"; "I have not prayed enough";
"I have been lacking in reverence in receiving the sacraments", and so on; for such accusations convey nothing
to your confessor as to the state of your soul; there is no
saint in heaven and no one on earth who could not say
exactly the same. Consider the particular reason you

77

have for making such accusations and then accuse yourself simply and openly of the actual fault, for example: you accuse yourself of not loving your neighbour enough, perhaps because you saw a poor person in great need and you did not help or console him when you could easily have done so. Say, then: "Having seen a poor man in need I did not help him as I might have done through negligence", or hardness of heart, or contempt, or whatever you know the real reason to have been. In the same, way do not accuse yourself of lack of devotion in prayer but simply of the fault which led to this, namely that you had distractions through your own fault or that you did not choose a suitable place or time, and so on. Do not be content with confession the mere facts of your venial sins but also the motive for which they were committed, for example, do not just say that you have told a harmless lie but that you did so to put yourself in a good light, to make a excuse for yourself, from obstinacy or just for fun. If you cheated in some game, say why: perhaps from a desire to win, and so on. Confess also how long you continued in your sin because this normally increases its gravity, there obviously being a great difference between a passing vanity which lingered in your heart for a mere quarter of an hour, and one which remained for several days. You must, then, confess the act itself, its motive and its duration, for though you are not bound to be scrupulous in confessing venial sins, in fact not strictly bound to confess them at all, yet if you really wish to purify youl soul and become devout you should be careful in making known to your spiritual physician the exact nature of your sin. If you have given way to anger, for example, say why. Suppose you took a joke in bad part because you disliked the person concerned when you would have accepted it from a friend; in this case you would say in confession, "I was angry with someone because I took something he said in bad part but only because I dislike him." It may be as well to repeat the actual words if that is necessary to make your meaning clear. By accusing yourself in this way, you not only make known your sins but also your evil inclinations, customs and habits, and the very roots of your sin, enabling your confessor to understand your heart better and apply the best remedies. Remember that, as far as possible, you must never disclose the identity of anyone who may have shared in your sin. Beware of those sins which often live and flourish unnoticed in your conscience so that you may confess them and be cleansed of them.[1]

Do not be too ready to change your confessor, but keep to the same one; go to him regularly and confess your sins quite candidly and sincerely. Every month or so reveal your inclinations, apart from any sin; the fact, for example, that you were troubled by sadness, felt joyful or avaricious and so on.

20. FREQUENT COMMUNION

IT IS SAID that Mithridates, the King of Pontus, derived such bodily strength from a drug he had discovered (and which was later named after him) that he was unable to poison himself when he wanted to avoid slavery under the Romans. Our Lord instituted the Eucharist, which truly contains his flesh and blood, so that *if anyone eats of this bread, he shall live for ever*.[2] Those who often receive this sacrament devoutly so strengthen their soul that it is almost impossible for them to be poisoned by

[1] Cf. Part III, 6, 27, 28, 29, 35, 36; Part IV, 8.   [2] John 6. 52.

any evil inclinations, for they cannot be nourished with this living flesh and at the same time be disposed towards spiritual death. In Eden, Adam and Eve were able to avoid bodily death by eating the fruit of the tree of life planted there by God. In the same way, those who eat the bread of life are able to avoid spiritual death. If we can easily preserve, for months, soft and corruptible fruits like cherries, apricots and strawberries, by conserving them in sugar and honey, it is not so strange that our hearts, no matter how frail and weak, may be preserved from the corruption of sin when conserved with the sugar and honey of the incorruptible body of the Son of God.

Christians who are damned, Philothea, will have no defence to make when the justice of their spiritual death is revealed to them since they could easily have avoided it by partaking of the food that he left for that purpose. "Why, wretched souls," he will say, "did you die when you had at your command the very food of life?"

"I neither praise nor blame," says St Augustine, "the daily reception of Holy Communion, but I recommend and encourage everyone to go to Communion every Sunday, so long as they are not attached to sin." I myself neither praise nor blame daily Communion without qualification, but leave it to the discretion of your confessor, the necessary dispositions being such a delicate matter that it is not prudent to encourage it for everyone. On the other hand, it is not a good thing to discourage everyone, for some may have the right dispositions; every case must be considered individually according to that person's state of conscience. It would be imprudent to encourage frequent Communion for everyone without distinction; it would be equally imprudent to dissuade anyone, particularly if he is following the advice of his confessor.

When St Catherine of Siena was criticized for her frequent Communion and St Augustine's words were quoted as an objection, she answered tactfully, "Since St Augustine does not blame it, I ask you not to blame it either and I will be satisfied."

But, Philothea, as St Augustine earnestly exhorts everyone to go to Communion every Sunday you should do so as far possible. Since you are not, I presume, in any way attached to mortal nor even to venial sin, you have the dispositions he requires, and more than he requires, for you are not even attached to the thought of sin, so it would be a good thing, with your confessor's permission, to go to Holy Communion even more frequently. He may advise against this, however, for various reasons, not, perhaps, concerning you, but those you live with.

If, for example, you are obliged to defer to others and they are so ignorant and irrational as to be disturbed and upset by your frequent Communions, it might be best on their account to go only once a fortnight; this, however, applies only when such difficulties cannot be overcome, nor must it be taken as a general rule; you must be guided by your confessor; though it is quite certain that those who wish to serve God devoutly should go to Communion at least once a month. If you are discreet neither spouse nor parents will stand in your way, for on the day you go to Communion you will fulfil all your duties and be particularly kind and gracious to them; when they find that it causes them no incovenience, they will not hinder you in any way unless they are perverse and unreasonable, in which case your confessor will advise you to give way to them.

With regard to those who are married; under the old law God discouraged creditors from exacting their debts on feast days, but not debtors from paying their debts when asked. To demand the payment of the marriage debt on the day of your Communion would be rather unseemly though to pay it, on the other hand, would be in no way unseemly but rather meritorious and so no hindrance to following one's devotion and going to Communion.

Certainly in the early Church, Christians used to go to Communion every day though married and blessed with many children; that is why I say that frequent Communion in no way inconveniences fathers, husbands or wives so long as prudence and discretion are observed.

Illness is no hindrance unless it causes frequent vomiting. To go to Communion every week you should be free from mortal sin, without attachment to venial sin and have a great desire for Communion; but to go every day you should, in addition, have mastered, for the greater part, your evil inclinations and even then you should go only on your confessor's advice.

21. RECEIVING COMMUNION

BEGIN your preparation the evening before by many acts of love, going to bed slightly earlier so that you may get up earlier the next morning. If you wake during the night fill your heart at once with loving aspirations, making your soul fragrant to receive our Lord who watches while you sleep, preparing countless graces and favours for you as you dispose yourself to receive them. In the morning rise in joyful anticipation of the happiness before you, and having been to confession, go, confidently yet humbly to receive the heavenly food which nourishes your immortal soul. Remain silent and still after saying,

Lord, I am not worthy;[1] open your mouth gently and moderately, lift your head sufficiently for the priest to see what he is doing, then full of faith, hope and charity receive our Lord in whom you believe and hope and whom you love.

When the bee has gathered the dew of heaven and the earth's sweetest nectar from the flowers, it turns it into honey, then hastens to its hive. In the same way, the priest, having taken from the altar the Son of God (who is as the dew from heaven, and true son of Mary, flower of our humanity), gives him to you as delicious food. When you have received him, stir up your heart to do him homage; speak to him about your spiritual life, gazing upon him in your soul where he is present for your happiness; welcome him as warmly as possible, and behave outwardly in such a way that your actions may give proof to all of his presence. If it is impossible to go to Communion, at least unite yourself to him spiritually by a fervent desire for the life-giving flesh of your Saviour. Your principal motive in going to Communion should be to advance, strengthen and console yourself in the love of God, receiving for love alone what is given for love alone. At no other time is our Lord more loving and more tender than when he, as it were, humbles himself and comes to us in the form of food that he may enter our soul and enter into intimate union with us. If you are asked why you go to Communion so often say it is to learn to love God, to be purified from your imperfections, delivered from your miseries, consoled in your troubles and strengthened in your weakness. Say that there are two sorts of people who ought to go to Communion often: those who are perfect since, being so well

[1] Matt. 8. 8.

disposed, it would be wrong if they did not approach the fountainhead of perfection; and the imperfect, in the hope of becoming more perfect; the strong lest they become weak, the weak that they may become strong; the sick to become well, the healthy to avoid sickness. Say that, for your part, because you are so imperfect, weak and sick, it is very necessary that you should often unite yourself to him who is your physician and the source of your perfection and strength. Say that those who are unencumbered with worldly affairs should often go to Communion because they have more opportunity; that those who have many worldly affairs should go frequently because they need it, nourishing food being necessary for those who have many labours and are heavily burdened. Tell them that you go to Holy Communion to learn how to receive it well, for we rarely do well what we do infrequently. Go to Communion often then, Philothea, indeed as often as you can with the advice of your confessor, and believe me, as mountain hares become white in winter because they neither see nor eat anything but snow, so by adoring and feeding on beauty, purity and goodness itself in the Eucharist you will become altogether beautiful, pure, and good.

PART THREE

THE PRACTICE OF VIRTUE

I. THE CHOICE OF VIRTUES

THE queen bee never goes forth to the fields without being surrounded by her subjects, and charity never enters our hearts without a retinue of virtues which it orders and directs as a captain his men, employing them, however, at different times, in different ways, and in different places.

A just man is like *a tree which is planted near the running waters, which shall bring forth its fruit in due season*,[1] for his soul, watered by charity, brings forth fruits of virtue, each one in due season. *Music*, says the proverb, *is out of place in time of mourning*.[2] To insist on performing acts of a particular chosen virtue on every possible occasion is a great defect, as in the case of certain ancient philosophers who wished to be always weeping or always laughing; and still worse, to criticize and blame those who do not do the same. St Paul says, *Rejoice with those who rejoice, mourn with the mourner*,[3] and, further, *charity is patient, is kind; charity feels no envy; charity is never perverse or proud, never insolent; does not claim its rights and cannot be provoked*.[4]

Some virtues, however, should be practised universally, either in themselves or in so far as they direct the practice of other virtues; for example, we seldom have the

[1] Ps. 1. 3.   [2] Ecclus. 22. 6.   [3] Rom. 12. 15.   [4] Cor. 13. 4, 5.

85

chance to practise fortitude, magnanimity or great generosity, but our whole lives should be coloured by the virtues of gentleness, temperance, modesty and humility. True, some virtues are more excellent, but none are more necessary—sugar is more excellent than salt, but it is not used to the same extent—and since we have to use these general virtues almost continually we should have an ample store ready to hand.

We should prefer the virtues which accord with our duty rather than our inclination. St Paula felt inclined to practise great austerities for the spiritual consolation they brought, whereas obedience to her superiors accorded more with her duty! That is why St Jerome blamed her for practising immoderate austerities against her bishop's advice. The Apostles, on the other hand, commissioned to preach the Gospel and distribute the bread of heaven to souls, were quite right to decide that the care of the poor, however excellent in itself, would hinder their mission.

Virtues differ according to our state of life; the virtues of prelates, princes, soldiers, married women and widows are all practised in a different way; though everyone should have all the virtues, they are not bound to practise them in the same way; on the contrary, everyone must practise in a particular way the particular virtues required of their state of life. With regard to the virtues which go beyond our duty, we should prefer the more excellent to the more spectacular. Comets usually seem greater and more striking than stars but only because they are nearer to us and of a coarser substance; in fact there is no comparison either in size or quality. It is the same with certain virtues which, because they are more striking and more material, are commonly more highly valued and preferred; for example, temporal almsgiving is perferred to spiritual; wearing a hair shirt, fasting, using the discipline and similar mortifications of the body, are preferred to gentleness, kindness and modesty and other mortifications of the heart, which in point of fact are more sanctifying. So, Philothea, choose those virtues which are best, not those which are only thought so; those which are most noble, not those which are most noticeable.

Everyone should make a point of practising some particular virtue, in order to concentrate and order his spiritual energies without, of course, forgetting about the rest.

A beautiful young girl, brighter than the sun, adorned like a queen, and with an olive wreath, appeared to St John, Bishop of Alexandria, and said: "I am the eldest daughter of the king; make me your friend and I will conduct you to his presence." Realizing that she symolized mercy to the poor, he practised this virtue so wholeheartedly that he became known everywhere as St John the Almoner. Eulogius of Alexandria longed to undertake some special work for God, but as he was not strong enough to become a hermit or take a vow of obedience, he received into his house a wretched man wasted with leprosy, that he might practise charity and mortification, and to do this more worthily he made a vow to honour and look after him as though he were his servant. Later, being tempted to separate, they asked the advice of the great St Antony who said, "My children, take care that you do not part, for both of you are near to death and if the Angel does not find you together, you run the risk of losing your crowns."

St Louis used to visit hospitals and look after the sick as though he were paid to do so; St Francis loved poverty above all, calling his virtue his Lady; St Dominic loved preaching, from which his order takes its name; St Gregory the Great, like Abraham, enjoyed entertaining pilgrims, and once entertained the King of Glory unawares; Tobias practised charity by burying the dead; St Elizabeth, though she was a great princess, delighted above all in humbling herself; St Catherine of Genoa, when she became a widow, dedicated herself to work in a hospital. Cassian tells a story of a devout young woman who went to St Athanasius to learn patience; at her request he made her look after a poor widow, peevish, ill tempered and unbearable whose constant scolding gave the girl sufficient occasion to practise patience and gentleness.

Among the servants of God then, some devote themselves to serving the sick, some to relieving the poor, to teaching children Christian doctrine, some to recovering those who are lost and gone astray, some to adorning churches and decorating their altars, while yet others seek to promote peace and concord among men. They are like embroiderers working in silk and gold and silver on various backgrounds, weaving countless lovely patterns like so many flowers; for those who undertake some particular devout work make it serve as a background for their spiritual embroidery, the practice of the various other virtues thus bringing order and unity to all their actions and affections so that their character is seen arrayed in robes of cloth of gold, in robes of rich embroidery.[1]

When troubled by some vice we must as far as possible practise the opposite virtue, making use of all the other virtues to this end. In this way we shall not only

[1] Cf. Ps. 44. 14, 15.

overcome our enemy but make progress in all the virtues. For example, if tempted to pride, or anger, I must force myself to practise humility and gentleness, making use of prayer and the sacraments, and exercising prudence, perseverance and temperance.

Wild boars sharpen their tusks by polishing them with their other teeth and sharpen them all in doing so; in the same way, a virtuous man seeking to perfect the virtue most necessary for his defence sharpens it by the practice of the other virtues, which in consequence are perfected and polished in their turn. It was in this way that Job, by concentrating on patience in the midst of the temptations which assailed him, perfected many other virtues. As St Gregory Nazianzen says, it is possible to attain the perfection of all the virtues by the perfect exercise of only one, quoting the example of Rahab who attained great glory through practising perfectly the virtue of hospitality; but this is true only in the case of a virtue practised perfectly and with fervent love.

2. FURTHER ADVICE ON CHOICE OF VIRTUES

St Augustine rightly points out that beginners in the spiritual life fall into various faults which are blameworthy according to the strict laws of perfection, yet praiseworthy in so far as they are a disposition to growth in devotion; for example, the servile fear which causes beginners to be scrupulous is praiseworthy in so far it foreshadows future purity of conscience while it would be blameworthy in those who are more advanced in the love of God which drives out fear.

St Bernard was, in the beginning, very strict and severe with those under his direction, and used to say from the first that they must forsake the body and come to him with the soul alone. In hearing their confessions he used the greatest severty, urging them so vehemently towards perfection that instead of helping to advance, to blame their faults, however slight, with he rather drew them back, for they lost heart when they found themselves being urged so fiercely up the steep path to perfection. Notice, Philothea that he chose this method because of his burning zeal for perfection, a zeal which was a great virtue, but nevertheless reprehensible, and in consequence God himself in a vision corrected him and in fused into his soul such a gentle, kind, loving spirit and merciful that he completely changed, blamed himself for having been so exacting and severe, and was so gracious and condescending to everyone that he became *all things to all men to gain them all.*[1]

St Jerome tells us that St Paula not only practised excessive bodily mortifications, but was so obstinate that she paid no heed to the advice of St Epiphanius, her bishop, when he tried to dissuade her; he tells us also that she gave way to grief, on the death of friends and relations, to such an extent that she nearly died hersef.

"It may seem," he wrote, "that instead of praising this saint I am blaming and critizing her; but I call Jesus to witness, whom she served and whom I desire to serve, that I err neither on one side nor on the other, but give a sincere account of her as one Christian of another; in other words, I write her history and not her panegyric and would point out that her faults are others' virtues."

He means that St Paula's faults and failings would be virtues in one less perfect, for there are some actions which may be considered as imperfections in those who

[1] 1 Cor. 9. 22.

are perfect but as perfections in the imperfect. So, Philothea, we must look kindly on those we see practising virtues in an imperfect way, since even the saints have done the same. As far as we ourselves are concerned, we must be careful to practise the virtues both faithfully, and prudently, taking the advice of Solomon not to lean upon our own prudence,[1] but upon those whom God has sent to guide us.

There are certain things which many consider as virtues but which certainly are not; for example, the ecstasies, raptures, states of insensibility and impassibility, levitations, and so on, mentioned in certain books, which promise to raise the soul to a purely intellectual contemplation, to an essential application of the spirit and to a supereminent life; but please notice, Philothea, that these perfections are not virtues but rather rewards given by God for virtue, foretastes of the happiness of heaven sometimes granted to man to awaken a longing for the complete bliss of paradise. Since these graces are in no way necessary for the true service and love of God, which should be our only aim, we should not aspire to them. In any case, some of these graces are such that by our own efforts we could never obtain them, for they are more passive than active; in other words things which we can receive, but not bring about in ourselves. After all we have only undertaken to become good and devout human beings and must concentrate on this. Should God lift us up to this angelic perfection, we should also be good angels, but in the meanwhile let us practise with simplicity and humility the little virtues, put before us by our Lord: patience, gentleness, the mortification of the heart, humility, obedience, poverty, chastity and thoughtfulness

1 Cf. Prov. 3. 5.

for others, forbearance, diligence and above all charity. Let us be prepared to leave exalted graces to exalted souls; we have not merited so high a rank in God's service and should be only too happy to be his servants, however humble our office; it is for him, if and when he sees fit, to promote us to more exalted offices.

Remember, Philothea, the King of Glory rewards his servants, not according to the dignity of their office, but according to the love and humility with which they carry it out.

Saul, looking for this father's asses, found the kingdom of Israel; Rebecca, watering Abraham's camels, became the wife of his son; Ruth, gleaning after the reapers of Booz, and afterwards lying down at his feet, was taken to his heart and became his wife.

The desire for external graces leads to illusion, deception and error; for it sometimes happens that those who imagine themselves angels are not even good men, and that their words and way of speaking are more exalted than their thoughts and deeds. However, we must never despise or criticize anything rashly, but rather praise God for raising others to the heights of perfection, while remaining humbly in our own way, which, though lower and less eminent, is safer and more suited to our insufficiency and littleness. If we continue in this way humbly and faithfully, God will lead us to truly great heights.

3. PATIENCE

PATIENCE *is necessary for you that, doing the will of God, you may receive the promise,*[1] says St Paul. Yes, for our Lord has said, *in your patience, you shall possess your souls.*[2]

[1] Heb. 10. 36. [2] Luke 21. 19.

To possess one's soul, Philothea, is man's greatest happiness and the more perfect one's patience the more perfect that possession. Remember that our Lord saved us by suffering and endurance and that we also must work out our salvation by suffering, by bearing affliction, by enduring injuries, contradictions and discomforts, as peacefully as we can. Do not limit your patience to any particular injuries or afflictions, but exercise it universally in all that God may send or allow to happen to you. Some people are willing to bear only honourable afflictions, like being wounded in battle or being a prisoner of war, being persecuted for one's religion or impoverished by some successful lawsuit; but such people do not love the affliction, only the honour which it brings. Those who are really patient and true servants of God are prepared to bear ignominious troubles as well as honourable ones. A courageous man is quite prepared to be despised, criticized and accused by the wicked, but his virtue is really put to the test when he is treated in this way by those who are good, by this friends and relatives. I think much more highly of the patience with which St Charles Borromeo accepted public criticism from the pulpit of a great preacher, belonging to a very strict order, than of the patience with which he bore the criticisms of others. In the same way that the sting of a bee is more painful than that of a fly, so the evils we suffer from good men are more hard to bear than those we suffer from others. It often happens that two good men, with the best of intentions, persecute and contradict one another because of some difference of opinion.

Be patient not only with regard to the essential affliction but also with regard to all those accidental inconveniences that go with it. Many people are quite prepared to be afflicted so long as they are not inconvenienced. "I would not mind being poor," says one, "if only it did not prevent me from helping my friends, bringing up my children properly, and from living as honourably as I should like"; another will say, "I should not mind being poor if only the wealthy did not think it was through my own fault"; another is quite prepared to bear slander patiently so long as no one believes it; others again are prepared to put up with some of the inconveniences of an evil but not with all of them. They say they are impatient, not because they are ill, but because they cannot pay for the proper treatment, or because their illness inconveniences others; but I say, Philothea, that we must bear patiently, not only illness, but the particular illness which God wills, where he wills it, amongst whom he wills it and with all the incoveniences that he wills; and so on with regard to other trials.

When any evil befalls you take the remedies within your power according to God's will; to do otherwise would be tempting God; but having taken such remedies leave the outcome to God's good pleasure with complete resignation. If they are successful, thank him humbly; if not, bless him with patience, which very few people do.

I agree with St Gregory: when justly accused of some fault humbly accept the accusations as more than deserved; when falsely accused, defend yourself calmly for the sake of truth and to avoid scandal; if the accusations still continue, remain quite calm and say no more, for having done your duty to truth, you should also do your duty to humility.

Complain as little as possible of your troubles, for normally speaking to grumble is to sin, self-love ever magnifying the wrongs we suffer; and above all never complain to evil minded gossips. If a genuine complaint is necessary for the sake of your own peace or to right the wrong, make your complaint to those who are peaceable and who love God; otherwise, instead of bringing peace to your heart, your confidants will disturb it all the more; instead of drawing out the thorn from your foot, they will only drive it deeper. Many people when they are sick, in trouble, or have been offended, avoid complaining or showing what they feel because they realize truly that it would indicate weakness and lack of generosity, but nevertheless they seek the pity and sympathy of others in countless little ways and desire that their patience and may courage be recognized. Perhaps this is patience, but it is a false patience, cloaking a very subtle form of vanity; of such people St Paul says they have *something to be proud of, but not in God's sight.*[1] A man who is truly patient does not complain of his troubles or seek sympathy. He speaks of them quite candidly, truthfully and with simplicity, without murmuring or complaining or exaggerating; if he is pitied he accepts this pity patiently and modestly, provided it is justified, thus preserving the balance between truth and patience, admitting what he suffers, but not complaining about it.

When you meet with contradictions in the practice of devotion remember our Lord's words: *A woman in childbirth feels distress, because now her time has come; but when she has borne her child, she does not remember the distress any longer, so glad is she that a man has been born into the world,*[2] for your soul has conceived the most noble child in the world, Jesus Christ, and you must suffer travail until he is formed and brought forth; but have courage, for when these birth pangs are over you will have ever-

[1] Cf. Rom. 4. 2.   [2] John 16. 22.

lasting joy at bringing such a child into the world and he will be truly brought forth when you have truly formed him in your heart, and in all you do, by imitating his life. When you fall sick, offer the sufferings, pain and weakness to our Lord, asking him to use them, uniting them with all that he suffered for you. Obey your doctor and take the prescribed remedies for the love of Christ, remembering the gall which he took for love of us. Desire to be cured that you may serve him, yet do not refuse to be ill that you may obey him, and be prepared to die should this be his will in order to praise him and share his joy. Bees live and feed on bitter food when making their honey; in the same way, we can never practise gentleness, patience or produce the honey from such excellent virtues more surely than when eating the bread of bitterness and living in the midst of afflictions. As the honey made from thyme, a bitter herb, is the best of all, so those virtues which we practise in the bitterness of the most wretched, lowly and abject afflictions are the most excellent of all. Often gaze with the eyes of your soul on Christ crucified, stripped, blasphemed, calumniated, abandoned and overwhelmed with every kind of trouble, sorrow and affliction; consider that your sufferings cannot possibly be compared in quantity or quality with his and that you will never suffer anything for him comparable with what he has suffered for you. Consider all the sufferings of the martyrs of old and those which so many people endure—far, far worse than yours—and say: "My pains are pleasures, my thorns roses, compared with the labours of those who, without relief or help or alleviation, endure a living death, weighed down with sufferings infinitely worse than mine."

4. EXTERNAL HUMILITY

BORROW *empty jars and do not stint thyself; then fill all these jars with oil,*[1] said Eliseus to a poor widow. Our hearts must be emptied of vain glory to receive the grace of God. The kestrel is able, by some secret power, to terrify birds of prey by its very cry and gaze, so that it is loved above all other birds by the doves who live safely in its company. In the same way humility terrifies Satan, and the graces of the Holy Spirit are safe where it dwells, hence the saints, and above all the King of Saints and his Mother, have always cherished this virtue above all the other moral virtues.

Vain glory is that which we accord ourselves for what is not in us, or for what is in us but not of us, and so not deserving of glory as far as we are concerned. To be of noble birth, to enjoy the favour of great men, to be acclaimed by the crowd, these things are not in us, but rather in our ancestors or in the eyes of others. Some people are proud and haughty because they ride a fine horse, or have a feather in their hat, or are very well dressed. This is obviously folly for if there is any glory here, it belongs to the horse, or the bird or the tailor. What mean hearts they have to depend on such things for their glory! Others think themselves great because they have a fine moustache or a well-trimmed beard; because of their curly hair, or their soft hands, or because they can dance or play or sing; to wish to enhance their value or reputation by such stupid frivolities is merely a sign of weakness. Others, whom we term pedants, wish that every one should honour and respect them, as students their master, because they have a little knowledge; others are

[1] 4 Kings 4. 3. 4.

vain about their beauty and imagine the world is at their feet; all this is very childish and futile and absurd. True good is known in the same way as true balm which is tested by being dropped into water, and is considered excellent and precious if it sinks to the very bottom; in the same way we know a man to be truly wise, learned, generous and noble, if these good qualities tend to humility, modesty and submission. On the other hand, the more conspicuously they remain on the surface the more they are to be distrusted.

Pearls conceived and nourished in wind and thunder have only a thin covering of pearl with nothing inside; in the same way, virtues and good qualities conceived and nourished in pride, vanity and ostentation only appear good and have no real depth or substance. Honours, high positions and dignities are like saffron which thrives and flourishes when trodden under foot. There is no honour in beauty when it gives rise to self-esteem. True beauty is unconscious of itself, while knowledge which makes us puffed up is no credit to us and degenerates to mere pedantry. Those who are oversensitive about rank, precedence and titles reveal thier own qualities as mean and contemptible.

Honour received as a gift is beautiful but not when sought after, asked for or exacted. When a peacock lifts and spreads its beautiful tail feathers in vanity it ruffles all there st, and its ugly parts are revealed; flowers which are beautiful when growing in the ground soon fade when picked. Those who smell the mandrake from afar and for a short time, find it sweet, but those who smell it close up for any length of time become stupefied and ill. In the same way, honours are pleasing when we enjoy their perfume at a distance, but only worthy of contempt if we set our heart on them and seek them avidly. To love and seek virtue tends to make us virtuous but to love and seek honours tends to make us contemptible and blameworthy.

The truly noble care nothing for such trifles as rank, honour and applause; they have other things to do and are above such pettiness of spirit. He who can have pearls does not trouble about the shells, so those who desire virtue are not eager for honours. Everyone indeed may accept and maintain the rank due to him without losing his humility, so long as he does so without affectation or contention. Those returning from Peru bring with them not only gold and silver but also monkeys and parrots because they cost little and there is plenty of room for them, so those who seek virtue bear with them their due rank and honour so long as this does not cost them too much care or attention or burden them with anxieties, distractions and contentions. This does not refer to public dignities nor those which pertain to particular and important occasions, for in such cases everyone should keep what belongs to him with prudence, discretion and a courteous and charitable spirit.

5. INTERIOR HUMILITY

As what I have said so far is rather wisdom than humility and as you desire, Philothea, that I should guide you further in this virtue, I will now do so.

Many people are frightened of thinking about the particular graces which God has bestowed on them lest they fall into vanity, and self-complacency; but in this they are surely mistaken for, as St Thomas says, the true way to learn to love God is to consider his favours; the more we appreciate them the greater will be our love, and as those bestowed upon us personally move us more deeply than those common to others, they should be considered more attentively. Certainly nothing can so humble us before God's mercy as the multitude of his favours, nor before his justice, as the multitude of our offences. Let us consider what he has done for us and what we have done against him; in the same way that we consider our sins in detail, let us also consider his graces, having no fear that the knowledge of his gifts will lead to pride, so long as we remember that what is good in us does not come from ourselves; mules are still clumsy brutes even when laden with a prince's precious personal possessions. What good have we which we have not received, and if we have received it why should we take pride in it? On the contrary, the lively consideration of graces received makes us humble and arouses our gratitude. If, however, the consideration of God's gifts does arouse our vanity, the infallible remedy is to consider our ingratitude, our faults and our wretchedness. If we consider what we have done when God was not with us, we shall realize all the more clearly that what we do when he is with us is not the result of our unaided mind and will; and while enjoying the possession of that good, we shall give the glory to God as its author. In this way our Lady acknowledged that God had done great things to her, humbling herself to glorify God, saying, *My soul doth magnify the Lord . . . because he has done great things to me.*[1]

We often say that we are nothing, that we are misery itself and nothing but refuse, but we should be very annoyed were we taken at our word and have this said of us by others; on the contrary we pretend to run away

[1] Luke 1. 46, 49.

and hide ourselves only that others may run after us and find us; we make a show of wishing to be the last and so take the lowest place at table but only that we may be asked to go higher. True humility is not ostentatious and speaks few words of humility, desiring not only to hide the other virtues but itself above all, and, were it lawful to lie, or give scandal, it would make a show of arrogance and pride to cloak itself and remain completely hidden and unknown. In my opinion, Philothea, you should refrain from expressions of humility or only use them when they really express your interior dispositions. Never lower your eyes without humbling your heart or make a show of wishing to be last unless it is sincere; this is such a universal rule that there must be no exceptions. I must add, however, that courtesy sometimes requires that we offer precedence to those who will certainly refuse it; this is not false humility, for the offer is an implied honour which we may rightly offer them in default of the honour itself; the same must be said of certain things we say out of honour or respect which strictly speaking do not seem to be sincere, yet they are true enough so long as we say such things with a true intention of honouring and respecting the person in question; though the words may seem slightly exaggerated there is no harm in using them if they are customary. Nevertheless it is preferable that our words should correspond as closely as possible with our sentiments, so that in all things and at all times they are simple and candid. A truly humble man would prefer another to call him a useless wretch than to say it of himself; at least he does not deny it, but freely admits it, only too glad that others should think the same as himself.

Many people say that they leave mental prayer to the perfect, being unworthy to practise it themselves; others say that they dare not go to Communion often because they do not consider themselves sufficiently pure; others say that they are so wretched and weak that were they to practise devotion they would bring discredit upon it; others refuse to use their gifts in the service of God or their neighbour lest being so imperfect they become proud or lose their own souls while trying to save others. All this is merely self-deception; it is not false humility but evil, because they are implicitly and subtly finding fault with the things of God, concealing their own opinions, inclinations and laziness under the cloak of humility. *Ask the Lord thy God to give thee a sign, in the depths beneath thee, or in the height above thee,* said the prophet to the wretched Achaz, and he replied, *No, I will not ask for a sign, I will not put the Lord to the test;*[1] under the pretext of great reverence for God, and under the guise of humility this unhappy man excused himself from accepting the grace offered by God, in his goodness, not seeing that it is nothing but pride to refuse God when he wishes to bestow his favours. It is our duty to accept what God offers, to obey with humility and comply with his desires as closely as possible. Now it is God's desire that we should be perfect, uniting ourselves to him, and imitating him as closely as we can. A proud and self-reliant man rightly fears to undertake anything, but a humble man becomes all the braver as he realizes his own powerlessness; all the bolder as he sees his own weakness, for all his confidence is in God, who delights to reveal his almighty power in our infirmity and his mercy in our misery. So with humility and confidence we should undertake whatever those who guide us deem useful to our progress. It is obviously foolish to think that we know

[1] Isa. 7. 11, 12.

what we do not know, and mere vanity to pretend to learning when we know perfectly well that we are ignorant; for my own part I would no more flaunt the knowledge I may have than pretend ignorance. When charity demands, we must freely and gently instruct our neighbour in what is necessary, not only for his instruction but for his encouragement; for humility, while it conceals and hides virtues to preserve them, will manifest them at the bidding of charity, to increase, develop and preserve them. Like that tree in the island of Tylus which closes up its lovely red flowers at night and keeps them closed till dawn, so that the inhabitants say that these flowers sleep by night, humility encloses and conceals all our virtues and perfections, revealing them only for the sake of charity, which, being not human but heavenly, not natural but supernatural, is the sun of the virtues and should govern them all, so that a humility which conflicts with charity is certainly false. I would wish neither to play the fool nor the wise man; humility preventing me from the one, simplicity and sincerity from the other, for as vanity conflicts with humility, so artificiality, pretence and affectation conflict with sincerity and simplicity. It is true that some great servants of God have pretended to be fools to humble themselves in the eyes of the world, but we should rather admire than imitate them; their own motives in this being so individual and particular that we cannot argue from them to our own case. When David exceeded normal propriety by leaping and dancing before the Ark of the Covenant, it was not because he wished to appear a fool, but because he was expressing outwardly, in all simplicity, the boundless joy in his heart; and when his wife, Michol, criticized him for acting in this way he was in no way disturbed but continued to express his sincere joy as before, only too glad to be despised for God's sake. When you are considered foolish and ridiculous for doing what the sincere devotion of your heart suggests, humility will turn this contempt to joy, the cause of contempt being in those who criticize you and not in yourself.

6. LOVE OF HUMILIATION

To proceed further, Philothea, I say that in all things you should love your own lowliness; but you will ask what this means? In Latin "humility" and "lowliness" are synonymous, so that when our Lady says in the *Magnificat, because thou hast regarded the humility of thy handmaid, all generations shall call me blessed,* she means that our Lord had looked with favour on her lowliness, disregard and insignificance in order to shower graces on her. There is, however, a difference between the virtue of humility and lowliness, for by lowliness we mean that littleness, ignominy and insignificance which is ours whether we think of it or not. The virtue of humility consists in knowing and freely admitting our lowliness, its perfection in being prepared not only to admit our lowliness, but to love and delight in it, not because we are lacking in courage and generosity but for God's greater glory and that we may think more highly of our neighbour in comparison. This is what I want you to do, and, to make myself quite clear, consider that of the evils we suffer some are humiliating, some honourable. Many people put up with those which are honourable but hardly anyone puts up with those which are humiliating. Consider the holy hermit shivering in rags; everyone honours his torn habit and pities his suffering but a poor workman, gentleman or lady in the same position would be mocked and despised; for their poverty is ignominious. A religious patiently accepts a harsh rebuke from his superior or a child accept a similar rebuke from its father; and everyone will call it mortification, obedience, wisdom; but if a gentleman or a lady acts in the same way, even for the love of God, it will be regarded as cowardice and lack of spirit. One man may have an ulcer on his arm, another on his face, the former suffers pain, the latter suffers contempt, embarrassment and humiliation as well. By patience we must love the pain, by humility the humiliation. Moreover, some virtues are humiliating while others are honourable; worldly people deprecate gentleness, simplicity and humility as small-minded and ignominious, while on the other hand they hold prudence, courage and generosity in high esteem. Some acts of a virtue are depised while others are considered honourable; for example, to give alms out of charity is considered honourable, to forgive injuries out of charity is considered by worldy people contemptible. Young men or women who avoid the excesses of evil company with regard to their conversation, games, dancing and the way they dress, will be mocked and criticized, their modesty being regarded either as priggishness or affectation; to love this is to love humiliation. I will give you another example; say I am going to visit the sick; if I am sent to the most wretched it will be a humiliation in the eyes of the world and so I will love it; if I am sent to someone important there is not so much virtue and merit in my visit; this will be a spiritual humiliation and I will love it as such. If I fall over in the street I am not only hurt but made to look foolish; I must love this humiliation. There are certain mistakes of which the only evil effect is our own humiliation; though humility itself does not demand that we should commit such mistakes on purpose, it does require that we should be undisturbed by them, for example, those acts of folly, impoliteness or inadvertence which we should certainly try to avoid out of courtesy and prudence, but which, once committed, should be willingly accepted for the sake of humility. I would go even further; if through anger or lack of restraint, we say anything unseemly, and offend God or those about us, we should be heartily sorry and as far as possible try to put it right; but at the same time we should accept the ignominy and contempt which this involves for us, and if it were possible to have one without the other, we should hasten to be rid of the sin, but humbly retain the humiliation. Even though we must love the humiliation which follows from an evil, we must do all we can to remedy the evil itself by taking the proper and lawful means, particularly if it is a serious evil. If I have some ugly blemish on my face I will seek to cure it, but not try to forget the humiliation it causes. If I have done something which offended no one, I will not make excuses, for, though in itself it may be a fault, its effect will not be lasting, and any excuse would concern only the ignominy, which humility cannot permit; but if, without thinking or out of stupidity, I have offended or scandalized anyone I will put it right by some genuine excuse, for its evil effects would be lasting, and charity demands its reparation. Moreover it sometimes happens that we should put an end to the humiliation for charity's sake, when someone else depends on our good name; in that case, while removing the humiliation to avoid scandalizing him, we must enclose and hide it in our heart to edify him. If you ask me, Philothea, which are the best

humiliations, I tell you quite plainly that the most profitable to us and the most pleasing to God are those which
come to us by accident or because of our state of life,
since we have not chosen them but have received them
from God, whose choice is always better than our own. If
we must choose, however, the best are the greatest, and the
greatest are those most contrary to our inclinations, provided they are in accordance with our state of life; for, to
say it once and for all, our own choice and selection spoils
or lessens nearly all our virtues. If only we could have the
grace to say with David, *Willingly would I lie forgotten
in the house of my God, so I might dwell no more in the
abode of sinners.*[1] God alone, Philothea, can give us this
grace, who lived and died *a byword to all, the laughing-
stock of the rabble,*[2] that we might be exalted.

Much of what I have said may seem hard when you
consider it, but believe me, when you put it into practice, it will be sweeter than sugar and honey.

7 · OUR GOOD NAME

MEN are given praise, honour and glory not for ordinary
but for extraordinary virtue: praise, to persuade others of
this virtue; honour, to indicate our own esteem; glory,
the radiance of their reputation which results from such
praise and honour, like a cluster of precious stones or
shining enamel. Humility forbids us to think ourselves
better than others or to desire the praise, honour and
glory due solely to excellence, yet it readily permits us
to follow the advice of the wise man and take care of
our good name,[3] because a good name relates to straightforward and upright intergrity of life rather than to ex-

[1] Ps. 83. 11.   [2] Ps. 21. 7.   [3] Cf. Ecclus. 41. 15.

cellence, and humility does not prevent us from recognizing such integrity in ourselves or from desiring a reputation for such. It is true that humility would despise a good name were it not required by charity, but because it is one of the foundations of human society and because without it we could do no good but rather harm to society by giving scandal, charity requires, and humility permits, that we should both desire it and do all we can to preserve it. The leaves on the trees are of no great value in themselves but they are nevertheless very useful to give the tree beauty and preserve its tender fruits. In the same way, a good name is not particularly desirable in itself, but it is very useful to embellish our lives and preserve our virtues, particularly those which are still weak and unformed.

The obligation of preserving our good name and of living up to it is a powerful and pleasant motive for generosity. Let us preserve our virtues, Philothea, for the principal and supreme motive of pleasing God but as those who wish to preserve fruits not only coat them with sugar but also put them in suitable jars so, though divine love is the principal preservative of our virtues, we may also use our good name as being very suitable and useful to that end.

Nevertheless, we must not be too eager, exacting or punctilious in doing so, or be too touchy or sensitive about it, lest we become like those people who take medicine for the slightest ailment and ruin their health completely in their efforts to preserve it; for to be too sensitive about our good name is to lose it, our touchiness making us unstable, obstinate or unbearable so that we merely antagonize our detractors. Disregard and contempt are usually far bettter remedies for insults and calumny than resentment, argument and revenge. Insults disappear before contempt but to resent them is in a sense to admit them.

Crocodiles hurt only those who are afraid of them, so slander only hurts those who are upset by it. To be too afraid of losing our good name indicates a distrust of its foundation which is a truly good life. Towns that have wooden bridges over great rivers are afraid that floods will carry them away, but those that have stone bridges are afraid only of torrents; so those whose lives are grounded in Christian virtue usually despise the outpourings of detractors, but those who are conscious of their weakness are upset by every little word. Indeed, Philothea, to wish to have a good name with everyone is to lose it with everyone, while to desire to be honoured by those whose sins render them infamous and dishonourable is to lose it deservedly. Reputation is merely a notice board on the door of virtue; it is the virtue that really matters; so if you are called a hypocrite because of your devotion, or a coward because you have forgiven an injury, it is no more than a laughing matter, for such statements are made only by foolish and empty-headed people. And even though we should lose our good name we should not turn away from path of virtue because of that, preferring the fruit to the leaves, in other words, the interior and spiritual good to any exterior good. We should be jealous of our good name but not worship it, and no more pander to the wicked than we would offend the good. A man's beard and a woman's hair are adornments; pulled out by the roots they will be hard to grow again; cut or shaved they will grow again more strongly and abundantly than ever; it is the same with our good name; if it is cut away or

109

even shaved off altogether by a slanderous tongue, which David likens to a *sharp razor*,[1] we should not be upset, for it will soon grow again, as beautiful as before and much stronger. But if we lose our good name through our sins, vices and evil life, it will be hard to grow again, since it has been torn out from the roots, for the root of a good name is goodness and integrity and only so long as these remain can it recover the honour it deserves. We must give up any idle habits, shallow friendships or unwise love affairs which harm our good name for it is of far more value than any pleasure these things may bring.

If anyone criticizes, teases or calumniates us for practising piety, advancing in devotion and progressing towards heaven, leave them to bay like dogs at the moon. If they cast a shadow on our reputation and so cut and shave the beard of our good name, it will soon grow again; the razor of slander will help our honour, as the pruning knife the vine, by making its fruit increase and multiply.

Let us fix our eyes on Jesus Christ crucified, serve him with confidence and simplicity yet with wisdom and discretion; he will take care of our good name, and if he allows us to lose it, it will be to give us a better one or advance us in humility, an ounce of which is more precious than a thousand times as much honour. If we are blamed unjustly, let us answer peacefully; if the calumny persists, let us keep humble, for by thus leaving ourselves and our reputation in God's hands we make it all the more secure. Let us serve God whether we are honoured or slighted, traduced or flattered, following the example of St Paul.[2] In this way we may say with David, *for thy sake, my God, I have borne reproach; shame hath covered my face.*[3]

[1] Ps. 51. 4. [2] Cf. 2 Cor. 6. 8. [3] Ps. 68. 8.

This does not, however, apply to crimes so dreadful and infamous that no one should allow himself to be falsely accused of them, if he can justly clear himself; nor does it apply to those whose good name is necessary for the edification of others. In this case theologians are of the opinion that we must peacefully seek to right the wrong.

8. GENTLENESS

THE holy chrism, traditionally used in the Church for confirmations and consecrations, is composed of olive oil mingled with balm, symbolizing, among other things, two virtues which shone out in our Lord and which he particularly loved and recommended, that by practising them ourselves we might better imitate him: *learn from me; I am gentle and humble of heart.*[1]

Humility perfects our relationship with God, gentleness our relationship with our neighbour. Balm, as I have already mentioned, always sinks to the bottom in all liquids and so represents humility; olive oil always floats to the top and symbolizes that gentleness which rises above all things and is pre-eminent among the virtues, being the flower of charity, which, St Bernard says, is most perfect when it is not only patient but also meek and gentle. Make sure, however, Philothea, that this mystical chrism, composed of gentleness and humility, is truly in your heart; for the devil deceives many into thinking they possess these virtues when, if only they examined their hearts, they would realize that they were deluded. Such people give themselves away when their outward show of gentleness and humility changes to arrogance at the slightest word of contradiction or the least insult. It is said that those who

[1] Matt. 11. 29.

have taken an antidote to snake bite, often called "St Paul's cure", do not swell up when bitten, provided this antidote is of good quality; in the same way, true humility and gentleness are an antidote to that swelling and fever which insults often arouse in our heart: but if we show ourselves proud, puffed up and angry when stung and bitten by slanderous enemies it is an indication that our humility and gentleness, instead of being true and sincere, are false and artificial. The great Patriarch Joseph sent his brethren home from Egypt with this one piece of advice: *Do not be angry in the way.*[1] I say the same to you, Philothea; this wretched life is but a journey to the happy life to come, so let us not be angry with one another on the way but travel together in gentleness and peace and friendship. Clearly, and without any exception, I say: Never be angry if you can possibly avoid it, nor open the door of your heart to anger on any pretext at all, for St James says quite simply and unreservedly: *Man's anger does not bear the fruit that is acceptable to God.*[2] Though we must constantly and courageously resist evil, and correct the faults of those in our charge, we must nevertheless do so peacefully and gently. Nothing appeases an enraged elephant so much as the sight of a lamb and nothing breaks the force of a cannonball so well as wool. A reprimand, however reasonable, loses its effect if given in anger, for anger befits tyranny rather than reason, and is hateful because it debases it. Princes accompanied by a peaceful retinue honour and rejoice their subjects, but when accompanied by troops, even for the public good, their visits are unwelcome and a cause of unrest, for no matter how well disciplined the troops, some disorder is inevitable, and someone is bound to suf-

[1] Gen. 45. 24. [2] James 1. 20.

fer. In the same way, as long as corrections, rebukes and punishments, however rigorous and exacting, are governed by reason, they are loved and well received; but when accompanied by anger, wrath and violence, reason is more feared than loved, and itself oppressed and harmed, by these accompanying sentiments. St Augustine writing to Profuturus says: "It is best to deny admittance even to just and reasonable anger, however slight, for once admitted it is hard to drive out; entering like a small shoot it soon grows into a branch." Once let the sun go down on our wrath, once let it stay the night, it will wake as hatred, and there will be little we can do to free ourselves from it. It finds a thousand false excuses to feed upon, for no angry man considers his anger to be unjust.

It is better, then, to try to live altogether without anger than endeavour to use it wisely and moderately, and if, because we are imperfect and weak, it takes us by surprise, it is better to drive it out at once than compromise, for with the slightest encouragement, like a serpent which slips easily through any hole large enough for its head, it soon makes itself at home. "How can I drive it away?" you may ask. You must at once, Philothea, gather your forces at its first appearance, without impetuosity or violence, but gently and calmly. In parliament and in courts of law it often happens that the ushers, in shouting for silence, only increase the tumult, and in the same way we often disturb our heart more than ever by trying to repress our anger violently, and cause it to lose mastery of itself.

After having made this gentle effort, follow the advice which St Augustine in his old age gave to the youthful bishop Auxilius; "Do what a man should and if it happens that you must say with the Psalmist, *vexation has dimmed my eyes*, turn to God saying, *Lord, have compassion on my distress*,[1] so that he may stretch forth his right hand and calm your anger." In other words, as soon as we see ourselves troubled by anger, we must seek God's help as did the Apostles when tossed by the wind and the storm upon the waters. He will command our anger to be still and there will be a great calm, but remember always that such prayer must be made calmly, peacefully and without any violence; and the same applies to all the remedies we take for this evil. As soon as you find you have fallen into anger, make up for it at once by some act of gentleness to the same person who has annoyed, you for as the best remedy for a lie is to unsay it at once, so the best remedy for anger is a prompt act of gentleness; fresh wounds, as they say, being more easily healed. In addition to all this, in times of tranquillity, when not tempted to anger, lay in a store of gentleness and kindness by speaking and acting, in great matters and in small, as gently as possible, remembering that the spouse in the Canticle of Canticles not only has *honey on her lips* and tongue but also *under her tongue*,[2] in other words, in her breast; for gentleness to our neighbour must not only be in our words but also in our breast, in other words, in our very soul. Not only should there be *honey* there but *milk* also, for this gentleness must not only have the fragrance and sweetness of honey with regard to strangers; it must also have the sweetness of milk with regard to those we live with and those about us; so they certainly fail in this, who seem angels in public but devils at home.

---

[1] Ps. 30. 10.   [2] Cant. 4. 11.

9. PATIENCE WITH OURSELVES

ONE of the best exercises of gentleness is to be patient with ourselves and our imperfections. Though it is reasonable to be displeased and sorry when we fall into faults, it should be without bitterness, anger or sulkiness. It is a great failing to be angry with oneself for giving way to anger, impatient with one's impatience and so on, since this only increases the original fault and, far from repairing it, it disposes the heart to fall again at the first opportunity. In any case, this sort of annoyance and bitterness with ourselves springs from self-love and leads to pride, for we are merely upset and disturbed at finding ourselves imperfect. Displeasure over our faults must be peaceful, unemotional and sincere. A judge whose sentence is based on calm reason will impose a more just penalty than if he judges with anger and impetuosity, for in the latter case, his judgement depends rather on his own feelings than on the crime itself. In the same way, we correct ourselves much better when we repent peacefully and calmly than if we do so with bitterness, over eargerness and passion, such repentance being based on our inclinations and not on our faults as they are.

For example, one who values chastity will be bitterly upset at the least lapse in this matter yet treat lightly a sin of grave slander; while one who hates slander will be tormented over a trivial offence, but think little of a great sin against chastity, and so on; their consciences being governed not by reason but by passion. Believe me, Philothea, a father's corrections administered with gentleness and affection are far more effective than those administered with anger and passion. In the same way, we should correct our heart gently and calmly after some fault, treating it with mercy rather than anger, and encouraging it to amend; this will arouse a much deeper and more lasting repentance than that which is anxious, fretful and violent. Say I had a great desire to avoid vanity and yet failed seriously, I would not reprove myself in this way: "Are you not wretched and hateful to be carried away by vanity after so many resolutions? Die of shame and never again lift your eyes to heaven, blind and shameless traitor to your God", and so on.

I would rather reprove my heart reasonably and with compassion as follows: "Well, my poor heart, here we are fallen again into that ditch we had resolved so firmly to avoid. Let us get up once more and leave it forever, imploring God's mercy and trusting that he will help us to be more steadfast for the future. Let us return to the path of humility, have confidence, and from now on let us be more on our guard; God will help us and we will do better." Then, I would make a firm and steady resolution not to fall again, asking the advice of my confessor as to the best means to this end.

If we find, however, that such gentle correction does not really move our heart, we may be more stern and severe, to humble it, provided that we end up by encouraging it to a calm confidence in God, following the example of David, who, finding his soul afflicted, encouraged it by saying: *Soul art thou still downcast? Wilt thou never be at peace? wait for God's help; I will not cease to cry out in thankfulness, my champion and my God.*[1] Lift up your heart, gently, then, after a fall, humbling yourself before God in the knowledge of your wretchedness, without being the least surprised that you have fallen. Weakness must expect to be weak, feebleness feeble, and

[1] Ps. 42. 5, 6.

misery miserable. Nevertheless, detest the offence against God with all your heart, then, with great courage and confidence in his mercy, go forward on the path of virtue which you have forsaken.

10. AVOIDANCE OF OVER-EAGERNESS AND ANXIETY

IT is one thing to manage our affairs with care, another to do so with worry, over-eagerness and anxiety. The angels take care of our salvation with diligence yet without any worry, anxiety or over-eagerness, for care and diligence accord with their charity while worry, anxiety and over-eagerness would not accord with their happiness; since care and diligence may be accompanied by peace and tranquillity but not worry, anxiety and even less over-eagerness. Carry out all your duties, Philothea, with care and diligence, for this is God's will, but as far as possible avoid being worried or anxious about them; never undertake them anxiously or eagerly. All eagerness disturbs our judgement, and hinders us from doing well the work we are so eager to do. When our Lord rebuked Martha he said: *Martha, Martha, how many cares and troubles thou hast.*[1] Had she been merely careful she would not have been troubled, but because she was over-eager and anxious, our Lord rebuked her.

Rivers which flow gently through the plains bear large ships and rich merchandise; rain which falls softly on the fields brings forth grass and corn; but rushing torrents are useless for shipping, and overflow their banks and ruin the land nearby, as violent rains lay waste the fields and meadows. Workd one with impetuosity and

[1] Luke 10. 41.

precipitation is never done well; we must make haste slowly; as the proverb says: *Ever the hasty stumble;*[1] hasty work is never good work. Drones make more noise and fuss than bees, but all they make is the wax, not the honey. Those who torment themselves with eagerness and anxiety do little and that badly. Flies trouble us by their numbers, not by their strength; in the same way, little things trouble us more than great by their very number. Accept all the duties that come your way peacefully, taking them in order, one by one; if you try to do them all at once they will weigh you down and disturb you so much that you will probably be unable to do anything. In all you do rely entirely on God's providence, on which all our plans depend for their success; nevertheless do your part peacefully, assured that, if you trust in God, the result will always be for the best even though it may not seem so to you. Act like little children who cling with one hand to their father while they gather strawberries or blackberries with the other. Hold fast with one hand to that of your heavenly Father while gathering and handling the things of this world with the other; turn to him from time to time to see if he is pleased with what you are doing, being careful never to let go of his protecting hand on the pretext of gaining more, for apart from him you will not take a single step without falling. In other words, Philothea, when your everyday duties do not demand any very great attention, look more on God than on your work; but when they are so important that they demand your whole attention turn to him from time to time, like sailors bound for port, who keep their eyes on the sky rather than on the ocean; in this way, God will work in you, with you, and for you, and your work will bring a blessing.

[1] Prov. 19.2.

11. OBEDIENCE

CHARITY alone makes us perfect, but poverty, chastity, and obedience are the three principal means of arriving at it. Poverty consecrates our possessions to the love and service of God; chastity our body; obedience our heart; while all three are rooted in humility. I will say nothing of these virtues as solemnly vowed, because that only concerns the religious life; nor will I say anything about them as vowed, simply, because, though such vows make them more meritorious, perfection requires only that they be practised. Vowed solemnly, they place us in a state of perfection; observed, they place us in perfection. All bishops and religious are in the *state* of perfection yet this obviously does not mean that they are *all* perfect. Strive then, Philothea, to practise these three virtues well, according to your state; without placing you in the state of perfection they will nevertheless bring you to perfection itself, for we are all bound to practise them, though not all in the same way.

Obedience may be either necessary or voluntary; by the former we obey our ecclesiastical superiors, i.e. the Pope, our bishop, parish priest and their delegates: the civil authorities, officials, magistrates and so on: also those over us in the home, i.e. father, mother, or in the case of servants, a master or mistress. We call such obedience necessary because no one is exempt from the duty of obeying those whom God has placed in authority over us, to direct and rule us in their own particular sphere. We must, then, of necessity, obey their commands; but to be perfect, we must also take their advice, and even fall in with their wishes, so far as charity and prudence allow. We should obey orders which are pleasing, for example, to eat, or take recreation, for though obedience seems no great virtue in such circumstances, it would be wrong to disobey; we should also obey in indifferent matters, for example with regard to what we wear, in taking one road rather than another in singing or being silent, such obedience being very praiseworthy; but our obedience will be perfect when exercised in difficult, unpleasing and hard matters. Obey meekly without answering back; readily and without delay; cheerfully without grumbling; but above all lovingly, for love of him who for love of us *accepted an obedience which brought him to death on a cross,*[1] and who, in the words of St Bernard, "preferred obedience to life."

To learn how to obey your superiors promptly, practise obedience to your equals, readily yielding to them without obstinacy or augument, in all save sin, and fall in willingly with the desires of your inferiors, in so far as this is reasonable, avoiding any imperious exercise of authority over them so long as they are good.

They are mistaken who think that they would obey readily if they were in a religious order, if they are stubborn and make difficulties in obeying those whom God has already set over them. Voluntary obedience is that to which we voluntarily bind ourselves and which is not imposed on us: for example, we do not choose our king, our bishop, our father or mother, sometimes not even a husband; but we may freely choose our spiritual director or our confessor.

St Teresa made a simple vow to obey Father Gratian over and above her solemn vow of obedience. Whether we do this or bind ourselves to obey anyone even without a vow, we call such obedience voluntary, because it depends on our own free choice.

[1] Phil. 2. 8.

We must obey our superiors in the particular sphere of their authority: for example, our civil rulers in all that concerns our public life; our bishop in ecclesiastical matters; father, master, husband and so on in domestic affairs; our spiritual director and confessor with regard to our spiritual life. Ask your spiritual director to prescribe your acts of devotion, for this will double their value and merit; for over and above their intrinsic value, Philothea, they will have the merit of being done under obedience. Blessed are the obedient, for God will never suffer them to go astray.

12. CHASTITY

CHASTITY is the lily of virtues and makes men almost equal to angels; nothing is beautiful unless pure and in man purity is chastity.

Chastity is synonymous with honour and makes us honourable; is synonymous with integrity and the lack of it with corruption; while its particular glory as a virtue of soul and body lies in its pure radiance.

It is never lawful to seek sexual pleasure in any way apart from marriage, which sanctifies such pleasure, and compensates for any spiritual loss it may occasion.

Even in marriage the intention must be pure so that despite any disorder arising from the pleasure, the will may remain upright.

The chaste heart can take no pleasure save in marriage ordained by heaven, apart from which it never voluntarily or deliberately delights in so much as the thought of its pleasure.

The first step to chastity, Philothea, is to avoid all unlawful and forbidden sexual pleasures taken either outside marriage, or, if married against the essence of marriage.

The next step is to forgo such lawful and permissible pleasures as are unnecessary or useless; while the third step is to be detached from even those pleasures inherent in marriage, for, though necessary, we must never set our mind and heart on them.

Chastity is necessary for everyone. Widows must practise it courageously by turning their backs on present or future pleasures and on the memory of past pleasures, however lawful, which awaken their desire.

St Augustine thought highly of the purity of his friend Alipius, who had forgotten and despised the pleasures of his youth.

Undamaged fruit can be preserved in straw, sand or its own leaves; but once bruised it can be preserved only in sugar or honey; similarly there are many ways of preserving chastity when it is unimpaired, but once violated it can only be preserved by the sugar and honey of a very strong devotion.

Virgins must practise a very simple and delicate chastity, avoiding all curiosity and despising all impure pleasures as fit to be desired more by asses and swine than by human beings, convinced that their purity is incomparably better than anything incompatible with it.

The devil tempts them to desire such pleasures, says St Jerome, by making them seem far more attractive than they really are: and they are troubled because what is unknown seems all the more desirable.

Like moths fluttering round a flame, until they perish in their curiosity to find out if it is as pleasurable as beautiful, many young people, dazzled by imagined delights, indulge their curiosity and fly to their ruin. They are more foolish than the moths, who have some excuse for being blinded by the beauty of the flame, for they persist in seeking what they know to be shameful and brutish. Contrary to what many think chastity is still very necessary to those who are married; and because it demands not abstinence, but selfcontrol is all the more difficult, just as it is more difficult to *be angry and sin not*[1] than not to be angry at all. As it is easier to refrain from all anger than to keep it within bounds, so it is easier to abstain from sexual pleasure than to observe moderation. It is true that passion is allayed in the holy freedom of marriage, yet, through weakness, this very freedom may be abused, and degenerate into dissoluteness.

As many rich people steal, not from poverty, but avarice, so many who married go beyond the lawful bounds of marriage, through lack of restraint and self-control. Strong remedies, no matter how well prepared, are dangerous, because an overdose does great harm. Marriage was in part designed as a remedy for passion, and though it is doubtless an excellent one, it is also a strong one, and so very dangerous if not used moderately. Since husbands and wives may often be separated by long illness or various circumstances, they must practise a twofold chastity : abstinence when apart, and moderation when together in the ordinary way.

St Catherine of Siena, in a vision, saw many suffering torments in hell for having violated the sanctity of marriage, not so much on account of the gravity of their sin in itself, for murder and blasphemy are far worse, but because those who sin in this way do not make it a matter of conscience and so persist in it for a long time.

Chastity, then, is necessary for everyone: *Your aim*

[1] Ps. 4. 5.

must be peace with all men, says St Paul, *and that holiness
without which no one will ever see God*.[1] The holiness to
which he refers according to St Jerome and St Chrysostom, is chastity; for, Philothea, only the chaste will see
God; *only the pure in heart will dwell in his tabernacle*,[2]
while *prowling dogs and wantons*[3] will be banished from
it. *Blessed are the clean of heart*, says our Lord, *for they
shall see God*.[4]

13. FURTHER ADVICE ON CHASTITY

TURN away at once from every temptation and attraction
to impurity, an insidious vice by which we are led from
bad to worse, a vice far harder to cure than to avoid.

Human bodies are like glasses, which cannot be carried when they touch one another without danger of
being broken; or like fruits which however sound and
fresh, are damaged by being brought into contact with
one another; even fresh water in a vessel becomes tainted
when touched by an animal.

Never allow anyone to touch you improperly, Philothea, either in fun or out of affection, for though such
harmless touches may not destroy your chastity they
destroy some of its freshness and beauty; but to allow yourself to be touched immodestly is the end of your chastity.

Chastity is rooted in the heart yet concerns the body; it
can be lost by means of the bodily senses, by thought,
or by desire.

It is impure to take pleasure in looking at, listening to,
speaking about, or touching anything impure; St Paul
says quite briefly, *As for impurity . . . there must be no
whisper of it among you*.[5]

Bees never alight on carrion and fly from its very smell.

[1] Heb. 12.14.   [2] Cf. Ps. 23. 4; 14. 1.   [3] Apoc. 22. 15.   [4] Matt. 5.8.
[5] Ephes. 5. 3.

124

The hands of the spouse in the Canticle of Canticles *drip with myrrh* which preserves from corruption; *her lips are as scarlet lace*, indicating the modesty of her speech; *her eyes soft as dove's eyes*, on account of their charity; her ears adorned with *golden ear-rings*, as tokens of her purity; her nose likened to the incorruptible *cedars of Lebanon*.[1]

To be devout, then, is to be chaste, pure and modest in hands, lips, ears and eyes, in fact in one's whole body.

Cassian tells us that St Basil said of himself one day, "I have not known a woman, yet I am not a virgin", meaning that there are as may ways of losing one's chastity as there are of being impure, and, depending on their gravity, they either weaken, wound or altogether destroy it.

There is a certain foolish and indiscreet intimacy and over familiarity which does not actually violate one's chastity yet weakens and undermines it, and tarnishes its radiance; but such intimacy and familiarity, when it becomes vicious and impure, seriously harms and endangers chastity, to say the least, and brings about its complete loss, in the end, if it leads to the taking of impure pleasure.

To lose one's chastity in this way is worse than losing it by fornication, adultery or incest, for compared with such sins Tertullian, in his book on chastity, refers to such pleasures as "monsters of iniquity and sin".

Cassian did not believe, any more than I do, that St Basil was referring to such pleasure, when saying he was not a virgin, but rather to impure thoughts which, without defiling his body, defiled his heart, the purity of which generous souls guard jealously.

Never mix with the impure, especially if they are

[1] Cant. 5. 5; 4. 3, 1; 1. 10; 7. 4.

shameless, as they usually are, for they can hardly even speak to anyone of their own, or of the opposite, sex, without contaminating them to some extent; being poisonous in eye and breath like basilisks.

On the contrary, mix with the pure and virtuous, think about holy things, and read the Scriptures *for the word of God is chaste*[1] and purifies those who delight in it, so that David compares it to *topaz*,[2] a precious stone which has power to allay the passions. Keep close to Christ Crucified, spiritually by prayer, and in reality by Holy Communion.

As those who rest upon the herb *agnus castus* become pure and chaste, so you, by resting your heart upon the pure immaculate Lamb of God, will be cleansed from all impurity and defilement.

14. SPIRITUAL POVERTY

BLESSED *are the poor in spirit for theirs is the kingdom of heaven,*[3] unhappy, then, are the rich in spirit for theirs is the kingdom of hell. The rich in spirit are those whose spirit is set on riches, the poor in spirit those whose spirit is not set upon riches. Halcyons make their nests like a ball, leaving only a small opening at the top; building them on the sea shore they make them so strong and impenetrable that even if the waves wash over them no water can get is; even in the midst of the sea they always float upright and weather the storm. Your heart, Philothea, should be like that, open only to heaven, and impervious to riches, and things that pass. If you should have riches, do not set your heart upon them; let it be always upright in the midst of earthly things and rise superior to them all.

[1] Cf. Ps. 11. 7.   [2] Cf. Ps. 118. 127.   [3] Mat. 5. 3.

It is one thing to possess poison, another to be poisoned. A chemist keeps poisons to be used on various occasions without being poisoned; these poisons being in his shop, but not in his body.

You may have riches without being poisoned by them, in other words, in your possession, but not in your heart. To be rich in fact yet poor in spirit is the great happiness of the Christian, for he has the use of the former in this world, and the merit of the latter in the next. Unfortunately, Philothea, no one likes to confess to being covetous; denying such baseness and meanness of heart, they excuse themselves on the ground that they must meet some great expense incurred on behalf of their children, or that prudence demands provision for their security. They never have too much money, but always find reasons why they should have still more. The most covetous, far from admitting their vice, will make a virtue of it, for avarice is like a raging fever; the worse it is, the more we become insensible to it. Moses saw the sacred fire which burned the bush without consuming it; it is otherwise with fire of avarice, which consumes and devours us without our being aware of it; in the midst of this fire, the avaricious person boasts of its pleasing coolness and counts his insatiable craving a natural and pleasing thirst. If you always desire passionately and with anxiety what you do not already possess, even though your desire is just, you will still be covetous, for those who desire to drink ardently, anxiously and without ceasing, even if it is only water, manifest their fever. I doubt, Philothea, if the desire to possess justly what others justly possess, can be justified, for it would seem that we desire to profit at the expense of others. Surely those who possess something justly have more

right to keep it than we to desire it? Why then should
we desire what we can only have by depriving someone
else? Even if this desire were just, it would seem to be
uncharitable; would we, ourselves, wish that others
might desire even justly what we justly wish to retain?
This was the sin of Achab who wished to possess Na-
both's vineyard justly, while, he, with more justice,
desired to keep it; because Achab's desire was passionate, anxious and persistent he offended God.

Never, Philothea, desire what belongs to your neighbour until he wishes to part with it, for in that case, your
desire would not only be just but charitable. You may
increase your riches and possessions, then, so long as you
do so not only justly, but peacefully, and with charity.
If you are still very much attached to what you already
have, too much concerned for your possessions, your
heart set on them, your thoughts occupied by them, fearful and anxious lest you lose them, it is obvious that you
still have the fever, like those who drink down water eagerly with unhealthy passion and pleasure. Remember, it is
impossible to take too great a pleasure in anything without being too attached to it. If your heart is too much
upset and troubled when you happen to lose some of
your possessions it shows, Philothea, that you are too
attached to them; for there is no clearer proof of being
attached to things than distress over their loss. Do not give
way to unbounded desire for goods you do not possess,
nor set your heart too much on those you have, nor be
too much distressed at losing them, and it will follow
that, though rich in fact, you are poor in spirit, and so
blessed, for yours in the kingdom of heaven.[1]

---

[1] Cf. Matt. 5. 3.

15. POVERTY IN THE MIDST OF RICHES

THE painter Parrhasius captured in a single ingenious portrait the varied and inconstant dispositions of the Athenians: their anger and courtesy; their injustice and mercy; their pride and humility; courage and cowardice. I desire, Philothea, to put together in your heart two things; riches and poverty; a great care, together with a great contempt, for the things of the world. Make sure that you make better use of your possessions than worldly people do. A king's gardener is more careful in cultivating the royal gardens than if they were his own, desiring that his services should please his master; so should we cultivate the possessions which have been given us by God. He wishes us to make good use of them and we please him by doing so; in fact, our care should exceed that of worldly people, for we are doing for the love of God what they are doing for the love of themselves.

Self-love is violent, over-eager and impetuous so that the care it inspires is full of anxiety, uneasiness and disquiet; the love of God, on the contrary, is gentle, peaceful and calm, and the care which it inspires, even in worldly matters, is gentle, calm and gracious. Let us take care of our possessions in this gracious way and even increase them, when a lawful opportunity presents itself, and in so far as our state in life requires it, for God wills that we should do so for love of him. Be careful, however, that you are not deceived by self-love, for sometimes it seems so like the love of God as to be mistaken for it. To avoid this, and to prevent the care for our possessions from turning into covetousness, over and above what I have already said, we must often practise real poverty in the midst of the possessions and riches given us by God.

Always give away willingly some of your riches to the poor, for we make ourselves so much the poorer in proportion to our gift. It is true that God will give it back, not only in the next world but also in this, for nothing makes us prosper in temporal affairs so much as giving alms; but until God does return it you will be that much the poorer, though such poverty is truly holy and rich. Love the poor and love poverty, and you will become truly poor, for we become like those we love.

Love makes lovers equal: *who is weak and I am not weak*,[1] says St Paul. He might equally have said: "who is poor and I am not poor with him", for love made him become such as those he loved. To love the poor, then, is to share their poverty; if you love the poor be often among them; welcome them to your house, visit them willingly, talk to them, be pleased to have them near you in church, in the street and so on. When speaking to them speak as one poor yourself, and as their equal; but, in helping them, give as one who possesses greater riches. If you want to go further than that, Philothea, be even poorer than they are, and how can you do that? Since *no slave can be greater than his master*,[2] serve them on their sick beds with your own hands, cook for them at your own expense, mend for them, be their laundress; such service carries with it more glory than a throne.

I cannot admire enough the zealous way in which St Louis, one of the greatest kings the world has seen, practised this counsel; and when I say great I mean great in every way. He often waited at table on the poor, whom he supported, and, nearly every day, invited three to his own table, often eating their leavings with incomparable love. When he visited the sick in hospitals, as he

[1] 2 Cor. 11. 29   [2] John 13. 16.

did often, he used to serve those with the most loath-some diseases, such as leprosy and cancer; went bare-headed, on his knees, to them, reverencing Christ in them, showing them a love as tender as that of a mother for her child. St Elizabeth, daughter of the King of Hungary, mixed freely with the poor and often, for re-creation, dressed as a poor woman among the ladies of her court, saying to them, "This is how I would be dressed if I were poor". This king and this princess, Philothea, were poor in the midst of their riches, yet rich in their poverty. Blessed are they that are poor in this way, *for the kingdom of heaven is theirs.*[1] *I was hungry and you gave me food; I was naked and you clothed me; take possession of the kingdom which has been prepared for you since the foundation of the world.*[2] Thus will the King of the poor, and the King of kings, speak on the day of judgement. Everyone has to experience poverty at some time or another; perhaps a guest may arrive whom we should like to entertain well and we have nothing to offer; perhaps we have need of our best clothes in one place and we have left them somewhere else; perhaps all the best wine in the cellar has gone sour and we have only inferior wine to offer; perhaps we find ourselves in some out of the way place in the country where everything is lacking, where there is no bed, no table, no attendance, perhaps not even a room; so, however rich we may be, we may often be in want of something. Welcome such occasions, Philothea, accept them willingly and bear with them cheerfully.

When impoverished by misfortunes, great or small, for example through storms, fires, floods, famine, rob-bery or lawsuits, then is the time to practise poverty by

[1] Matt. 5. 3.   [2] Ibid. 25. 34, 36.

bearing your losses calmly with patience and constancy. Both Esau and Jacob came to their father, their hands covered with hair. In the case of Jacob, it was attached to his gloves, not to his flesh, and so could be removed without hurting him; but, in the case of Esau, it was his own so that, if anyone tried to tear it off, it would have caused him great pain and he would have cried out and resisted.

When our hearts are attached to our possessions we complain and are troubled and impatient if storm, thief or impostor take any of them away; but, if we are only attached to them for God's sake, we are not upset by their being taken away, nor do we lose any of our peace of soul. In this lies the difference between animals and men with regard to their clothing, for that of the animals is attached to their flesh while that of men is such that it may be put on and taken off at will.

16. RICHNESS OF SPIRIT IN THE MIDST OF POVERTY

If, Philothea, you are poor in reality, be poor also in spirit. Make a virtue of necessity and profit by this precious jewel, whose richness and beauty are none the less for being hidden in this world. Have patience, for you are in good company; our Lady, our Lord, the Apostles and so many of the saints, both men and women, have been poor, despising the riches they might have had. Many rich persons have ardently sought, in the face of great opposition, poverty, in cloister or hospital; for example, St Alexis, St Paula, St Paulinus, St Angela and many others, while in your case, Philothea, poverty, showing you more courtesy, has entered your house without your having to seek it and without any trouble. Embrace poverty as a dear friend of Christ, who was born, lived and died in the company of poverty, which nursed him all his life.

Two great advantages, rich in merit, follow from your poverty, Philothea; the first advantage is that it is not of your own choice, but through the will of God; whatever we receive in this way is always very pleasing to him, so long as we receive it willingly and lovingly, for where there is less of our will there is more of his. To accept God's will entirely and with simplicity sanctifies our suffering.

The second advantage lies in the fact that it is true poverty. A poverty which is praised, esteemed, helped and assisted has something of richness about it, or at least is not absolute poverty, as is that which is despised, rejected, scorned and abandoned, for that is poverty indeed.

The poverty of people in the world normally comes into this category, for since they are not poor of their own choice but of necessity, people make little of it; in this sense their poverty exceeds that of religious which, however, has an excellence of its own, and is more commendable, on account of the intention for which it was chosen, and because sanctified by a vow. Never complain, then, Philothea, of your poverty, for we only complain of what displeases us; in which case, you are not poor in spirit, but rich because attached to riches. Do not be troubled if you fail to receive all the help you need, for there lies the excellence of poverty. To desire poverty without its inconveniences is to desire both the honour of poverty and the convenience of riches. Do not be ashamed of your poverty or of asking alms in charity; accept help with humility, a refusal with meekness.

Meditate often on The Flight into Egypt, and consider the contempt, poverty and misery our Lady had to endure; imitate her and you will be rich in your poverty.

17. FOOLISH FRIENDSHIPS

LOVE is the soul's dominant passion; it rules all the movements of the heart, making them its own, and making us like that which we love. Take care, then, Philothea, to admit no evil love lest you soon become evil yourself. Love which goes with friendship is most dangerous, for some love may exist without mutuality, but since friendship is entirely dependent on this it cannot exist without our becoming like the person we love.

Not all love is friendship for one can love without being loved; in which case there is love without friendship, friendship demanding mutual love. Nor is it enough that it be mutual; both must also know it to be such, otherwise there may be love but still not friendship. There must also be some kind of communication on which the friendship is based.

There are as many kinds of friendship as there are grounds for it, and things to share. If such things are false and useless then so is the friendship; if they are good, then so is the friendship, taking its quality from that of the things shared.

As the best honey is derived from the choicest flowers, so love which is based on the sharing of really good things is the best. In Heraclea in Pontus there is a poisonous honey gathered from the aconite which bemuses those that eat it; so friendships based on the sharing of false and evil things are altogether false and evil. The mutual sharing of sexual pleasure, as such, can no more be called friendship than the same thing between animals. If this were the only thing shared in marriage there would be no friendship, but because there is also a sharing of life, of work, of possessions of affection, and of indissoluble fidelity there is a true and sacred friendship. As a friendship based entirely on sensual pleasure is unworthy of the name, so also is that friendship which is based on superficial qualities. By sensual pleasure I refer to the pleasure experienced by the senses, in looking at someone who is beautiful, for example, in listening to a charming voice, in touching and so on; by superficial qualities I mean such accomplishments, and characteristics which foolish people count as virtues and perfections.

Listen, for example, to the talk of most young girls who do not hesitate to say: "Such a man is very accomplished, has many perfections, for he dances well, is very good at games, is well dressed, sings well; he is so nice to talk to, and so good looking", the most amusing being considered the most accomplished. As all these things depend upon the senses, the friendships based on them are sensual and frivolous, and should be called folly rather than friendship; and this applies to most of the friendships of young people which are based on a moustache, beautiful hair, smiling eyes, fine clothing and frivolous talk. Such friendships befit only the young and unfledged lover whose judgements are unformed; transitory, they melt away like snow in the sun.

18. FLIRTATIONS

SUCH foolish friendships formed with persons of the opposite sex, without any intention of marrying, are called flirtations; abortive imitations, frivolous and imperfect, they do not deserve the name of friendship or of love, but merely entangle the hearts of men and women with vain and puerile affections based on the stupid grounds and miserable pleasure I have mentioned already.

Though such affairs usually end by being swallowed up in impure lust and sensuality, that is not the original intention of those who indulge in them, or they would come in the category of blatant impurity rather than of mere flirtations.

Such folly may continue for years without any direct breach of bodily chastity, merely dissipating the heart with wishes, desires, sighs, expressions of love and so on, for varying motives. Some, merely to ease their heart by loving and being loved, follow their amorous inclinations, their choices determined by those inclinations and instincts alone, and become hopelessly entangled in the wretched web of an affair with someone who attracts them at first sight, without considering his character or reputation.

Others are ensnared through vanity, winning and binding hearts by love for the mere glory of it, and for this very reason casting their net and setting their snares in high, illustrious and exclusive circles.

Others, again, are led by their inclinations but by vanity as well, so that though their heart tends to love, they will only engage in an affair if it redounds to their own glory.

Such relationships are evil, foolish and empty: evil because they end up in sins of the flesh and deprive God, wife or husband, of the heart and the love which is theirs by right; foolish because groundless and unreasonable; empty because fruitless, yielding neither peace nor honour; on the contrary they are a waste of time, they compromise our good name, while their only pleasure lies in vague hopes and the eager anticipation of they know not what; for these weak and foolish people are sure that their mutual expressions of love must have some value or other, though they do not know what it is, and so are never satisfied, their heart forever disturbed by endless suspicion, jealousy and anxiety.

St Gregory Nazianzen expressed himself very well on this subject, addressing vain women, though his words apply equally well to men:

"Your natural beauty suffices your husband, but if flaunted before many men like a net to catch a flock of birds, what will be the result?

"You will be pleased by those whom your beauty pleases, returning glance for glance, gaze for gaze, then smiles and little words of love, guarded at first, but soon becoming more familiar until you are openly making love.

"Take heed, my tongue, lest I mention what follows! but I will say this; everything such foolish lovers say or do is an incitement to evil; one thing inevitably leads to another in these wretched flirtations as one piece of iron drawn by a magnet, draws others in its turn."

This great bishop's words are certainly wise. What are you trying to do? To give love to someone? But you cannot give your love to anyone without necessarily receiving his in return; in this game, to capture is to be captured.

The herb *aproxis* is said to burst into flames at the very sight of fire, and our hearts are the same; they are inflamed at the sight of a heart on fire with love for them. Some say they wish only to taste a little of this love—but they are deceived—the fire is more consuming than it appears; seek but a spark and to your amazement you will find your whole heart consumed in a moment, your resolutions reduced to ashes and your good name to smoke·

The wise man cries out *who will pity a snake-charmer struck by a serpent.*[1] I echo his words: Senseless fools—do you think you can charm and master love at will? Play with it and you will be badly bitten and stung—and what will others say? They will laugh and make fun of your false confidence in attempting such folly, in taking to your bosom the dangerous serpent which stung you and by which your soul and honour have been poisoned.

What blind recklessness to risk one's soul for stakes so trifling! It is our soul that counts with God, Philothea, our soul for its will and our will for its love; and we have so little love to spare, are so far from having all the love we need with which to love God; yet in our wretchedness we lavish it on vain and useless trifles as if we had abundance.

God asks all our love for having created, preserved and redeemed us and will call us strictly to account for having squandered it; if *every thoughtless word*[2] is to be reckoned what of our thoughtless, reckless, foolish and base love affairs!

Vineyards and fields are greatly harmed when a walnut tree is planted in them for by its very size it absorbs all the moisture of the soil, leaving it barren; the deep shade of its dense foliage and its fruit tempts passers-by who trample down and ruin everything nearby.

So the soul is harmed by flirtations which absorb its interests and its life to such an extent that it is barren of good works; frequent meetings, dalliance and philande-

---

[1] Ecclus. 12 13.   [2] Matt. 12. 36.

ring eat up all its leisure, while so many temptations, distractions and suspicious rush in that one's whole heart is trampled down and devastated.

Such flirtations then exclude heavenly love, and the fear of God, enervate the soul and damage our reputation; they are the sport of society but the bane of the heart.

19. TRUE FRIENDSHIP

LET your charity extend to everyone, Philothea, but limit your friendship to those with whom you can share virtuous things; the more perfect they are, the more perfect will your friendship be. Share knowledge and your friendship will be most praiseworthy; mutual help in the practice of virtues, prudence, discretion, fortitude and justice, will be more praiseworthy still; but friendship based on charity, devotion and Christian perfection will be most praiseworthy of all; it will be excellent, because it comes from God, tends to God and is founded on God; excellent because it will last for ever in God. What a wonderful thing it is to love on earth as we shall love in heaven, to cherish one another in this world as we shall for ever in the next. When I speak of charity here, I am not referring to the love we should have for everyone, but to a spiritual friendship by which two or more people share their devotion and aspirations with each other, and become one in spirit, so that they can truly say, *Gracious the sight, and full of comfort when brethren dwell united.*[1]

The delicious balm of devotion flows continually from one heart to another so that we may say God has bestowed upon this friendship his *benediction and life everlasting.*[2]

[1] Ps. 132. 1. [2] Ibid. 4.

139

All other friendships, to my mind, are but shadows compared with this; and the chains which bind them together are like glass or jet, compared with those of charity, which are made of gold. Do not make any other kind of friendship, that is, of your own choice, for you should not forsake or neglect for new friends those to whom you are bound by nature or duty: relatives, benefactors, or neighbours.

Many may tell you that we should avoid all particular friendships because they occupy our heart, distract our mind and lead to jealousy, but such advice is mistaken, based on the fact they have seen in the works of many holy and devout writers that particular friendships and excessive feelings of affection are very harmful to those leading the religious life, and they imagine that this applies to everyone; but we must make a clear distinction.

In a well-ordered monastery, the common aim of all tends to devotion, so that particular friendships are unnecessary; in which case, to seek from an individual what should be sought from the whole is to give in to partiality; but it is necessary for those who seek true virtue in the world to form good and holy friendships, to encourage, help and guide one another on the path of virtue. Those who travel across a plain need not assist one another, but those who travel on rough and slippery roads must cling to each other for security. So those who belong to a religious order need no particular friendships while those who live in the world do need them, that they may help one another to travel safely despite the difficulties of their path. Those in the world have different aims and ideals so that we must form our friendships with those who share our aim. Such partiality is justified, making distinction only between good and evil, between the sheep and the goats, the bees and the hornets; a most necessary distinction. No one can deny that our Lord loved St John, Lazarus, Martha and Mary with particular tenderness and affection, for the Gospels tell us so. We know too that St Peter had a particular love for St Mark and St Petronilla, as had St Paul for Timothy and St Thecla; St Gregory Nazianzen often boasts of his incomparable friendship with St Basil and says, "It seemed as though we two had but one soul; and though we must not hold that all things are in all things, yet you must believe that we were two in one and each in the other, having the one aim: to practise virtue and to centre our life on eternity, thus passing beyond this mortal life while still in the world."

St Augustine tells us that St Ambrose had an incomparable love for St Monica, because of the rare virtues he saw in her; while on her part she loved him as an angel of God; but I will waste no more of your time on something so obvious. St Jerome, St Augustine, St Gregory, St Bernard and all the greatest servants of God have had very particular friendships without any detriment to their perfection.

St Paul when reproaching the Gentiles for their disorders, accuses them of being *without love;*[1] in other words, without friendship; and St Thomas, like all good philosophers, holds friendship for a virtue; and he refers to particular friendship since he holds that perfect friendship cannot extend to many persons. Perfection, then, does not consist in having no friendships at all but in having only those which are good and holy and sacred.

[1] Rom. 1. 31.

20. THE DIFFERENCE BETWEEN TRUE AND
FALSE FRIENDSHIP

REMEMBER, Philothea, that the poisonous honey of Heraclea looks so much like true honey that there is a danger of mistaking one for the other, or of eating them mixed together, when the wholesome properties of the one would not counteract the harmful properties of the other. We must take care not to be deceived in our friendships, especially when contracted with someone of the opposite sex, no matter on what pretext; for the devil often misleads those in love; their love may begin by being virtuous, but unless they are prudent it will become mixed with frivolous love, then with sensual love. Even spiritual love is dangerous, unless we are very careful; since there is less room for deception, its very purity and whiteness making it easier to detect the impurities which the devil tries to mix with it, he undertakes his task all the more subtly and insinuates impurities without our noticing. Worldly friendship may be distinguished from sacred friendship as the honey of Heraclea is distinguished from true honey; as the former tastes sweeter than ordinary honey because of the added aconite, so worldly friendship is usually flavoured with sweet words and flattering praise of beauty, gracefulness and physical qualities; while the language of holy friendship is simple and frank, full of praise only of the power and graces of God on which it is based.

The honey of Heraclea makes the head dizzy; false friendships do the same for the soul, causing us to falter in virtue and devotion, carried away by lingering glances, sensual caresses, long sighs, murmurs about not being loved, little poses which are intentionally alluring, flattery, the solicitation of kisses and other improper attentions and intimacies, quite certain forerunners of chastity's decay.

In the case of holy friendships, on the contrary, glances are sincere and modest; embraces pure and innocent; sighs only for heaven; familiarity is purely spiritual, its laments only concern failure in divine love; all of which betokens chastity.

As the honey of Heraclea affects our sight, so worldly friendships affect our judgement, causing those involved to clothe vice with virtue, to think their excuses, pretexts and extenuations true and reasonable; to fear the light and love the dark; while holy friendships make us clear-sighted and we are quite prepared to profess them openly in virtuous company.

Finally, as the honey of Heraclea leaves a bitter taste in the mouth, so false friendships dissolve, ending in sensual words and base requests which, if refused, lead to insults, calumny, deception, bitterness, disquiet and jealousy, and often end in madness; while pure friends make us consistently modest, kind and courteous, and develop into that pure and perfect spiritual union which reflects the union of the blessed in heaven.

St Gregory Nazianzen says that the peacock incites peahens to lechery when it spreads its tail and struts and calls; so we may be sure that a man who comes dressed up, strutting like a peacock, to whisper flattering and coaxing words in some woman's ear, is only bent upon seducing her.

If honourable, she will *turn a deaf ear and will not listen to the snake-charmer's music* or to the peacock's cry, *skilful enchanter though he be,*[1] but, should she listen then her heart is already lost.

[1] Ps. 57. 5.

Those who put on airs, indulge in looks, and caresses, and say things which they would not like their father or mother, husband, wife or confessor to overhear, are clearly not discussing matters of honour and conscience!

Our Lady was troubled when an angel appeared to her in the guise of a man, since she was alone, and his praise excessive, though it were from heaven; if she who is purity itself can so fear an angel in human form, should not one who is weakness itself fear a man whose praises are sensual and earthly, even though he seems an angel?

21. REMEDIES FOR FALSE FRIENDSHIPS

WHAT are the remedies for all these flirtations, love affairs and worse? The first thing is to turn your back resolutely on such follies from the very beginning. Hasten to Christ Crucified and place his crown of thorns about your heart to keep out those *little foxes*.[1] Beware of coming to terms with the enemy, saying, "I will not do what he says, but only listen; will lend him my ears but refuse him my heart."

In God's name, Philothea, be ruthless in this matter; your heart and your ears are so closely associated that it is as impossible to prevent love from flowing down from your ears into your heart as to stay a torrent once it begins to flow from the mountain tops. Aristotle denies the theory of Alcmæon, that goats breathe through their ears instead of through their nostrils, but it is certain that our heart breathes in the ideas of others through our ears, as it breathes out our own through our lips. So we must guard our ears carefully lest our heart be tainted by the evil breath of fools.

[1] Cant. 2. 15.

Do not listen to any evil suggestions, no matter what the pretext; this is one case when you can be abrupt and discourteous with impunity.

Remember that your heart is dedicated to God; your love belongs to him; to retract even a little of it would be a sacrilege; you should rather re-dedicate it all to him by a thousand resolutions and promises, sheltering in them like a stag within its covert; God will help you, protecting your love with his own that it may be all his.

If you are already in the toils of such an affair, the task of freeing yourself will not be easy: place yourself in the presence of God, acknowledge your weakness, wretchedness and vanity, then renounce your foolish love with all your heart and resolve absolutely to take no further part in the follies of the game of love.

I would strongly recommend you to separate if possible; two people stung by the dart of love, like two people bitten by the serpent, are more easily cured apart, while a change of scene greatly helps to alleviate the distressing pangs of sorrow or of love.

St Ambrose, in his book on penance, speaks of a young man who returned from a long voyage completely cured of a foolish infatuation and so changed that, when his mistress met him with these words, "Don't you know me? I am still the same", he replied, "Yes, but I am not" . . . a happy change brought about by their separation. St Augustine tells us that to alleviate his sorrow at the death of his friend in Tagaste, he left there and went to Carthage.

But what if it is not possible to go away? All private meetings, all secret talks, all loving glances and smiles, everything which feeds the smouldering fire of mutual love must be renounced entirely.

If a meeting is unavoidable let it be to make known, briefly, courageously and in no uncertain terms, your sworn resolution to part for ever.

To all who have become entangled in the fetters of such an affair I cry out, "Rend and tear them away; do not waste time in trying to unravel them; simply sever them. Do not try to unfasten them; these bonds are valueless so do not hesitate to break and slash them away with no consideration at all for a love which conflicts with the love of God."

Your fetters cast away, may there not yet linger memories and traces of your love within your heart? Not if you detest the evil, Philothea, as much as it deserves, for then your only feeling will be one of sorrow for the baseness of your love and for everything that went with it, your heart free of all the love for that person save that which is for God's sake.

If through the imperfection of your repentance, some evil inclinations remain in your heart, then practise spiritual retirement as I have taught you, entering the shrine of your soul as often as possible, renouncing those inclinations with all your heart by countless acts of sorrow and of love; give yourself more seriously to spiritual reading, go to confession and Communion more frequently, and discuss your feelings and temptations quite frankly and in all humility with your confessor or with a wise and faithful friend, and be sure that, so long as you persevere, God will deliver you from them all.

"Is there no ingratitude", you may ask, "in breaking up a friendship so ruthlessly?" Such ingratitude, were it so, would win you a blessing since it would be pleasing to God; but I say in his name that it is not so. Rather do you confer a great benefit on your lover by sundering the fetters which bound you both equally, and though your lover may not appreciate this benefit at first, the realization will come before long, and together you will sing in gratitude, *O Lord, thou hast broken the chains that bound me, I will sacrifice in thy honour, and call upon the name of the Lord.*[1]

22. FURTHER ADVICE ON FRIENDSHIP

FRIENDSHIP can neither begin nor continue without the sharing of mutual interests and it often happens that this sharing extends unnoticed to many other things, particularly when friends think highly of one another for then they open their hearts more easily to one another's ideas and influence, whether good or bad.

Bees which gather the honey of Heraclea seek only honey, yet, without noticing, they also draw in the poisonous qualities of the aconite from which they gather it. So, Philothea, we must practise the advice attributed to our Lord, "Be good money-changers"; in other words, do not accept counterfeit money with the good nor debased gold with the pure; *separate worth from dross*![2] for there is hardly anyone without some imperfection. Why should we receive, indiscriminately, the faults and imperfections of a friend together with his friendship? True we must love our friends in spite of their imperfections, but we must not love or receive their imperfections, friendship requiring that we share the good but not the evil.

As those who get gravel from the river Tagus sift out and keep the gold while leaving the gravel on the bank, so should we separate the gravel of imperfections from the

[1] Ps. 125. 7.   [2] Jer. 15.19.

blessings of friendship, and not allow them to enter our soul.

St Gregory Nazianzen says, it is true, that many who loved and admired St Basil were led to imitate even his exterior imperfections, his way of speaking slowly, thoughtfully and absentmindedly, the shape of his beard, and the way he walked; and we see husbands, wives, children and friends acquiring one another's imperfections through their very love and companionship; but this is wrong, for everyone has enough imperfections of his own without adding those of others, and friendship does not require this; on the contrary it obliges us to free one another all we can from our imperfections; to bear patiently with them, but not encourage them, much less make them our own. This refers only to imperfections, in the case of sins we must not even tolerate them in a friend; it is a poor or false friendship that can allow a friend to perish without help, that dare not lance an abscess to save his life; true friendship cannot co-exist for long with sin, for it ruins that friendship, as the salamander puts out the fire in which it takes refuge. Friendship, can put on occasional sin to flight at once by correction, but if the sin is habitual the friendship perishes for it can only exist with true virtue. How much less should we sin for the sake of friendship; the friend who would lead us into sin is an enemy. He who would ruin his friend deserves to lose his friendship. The most certain indication of a friendship being false is when it endures with a vicious person, whatever his vice, for a vicious friend can make only a vicious friendship; since it is not based on true virtue it must be based upon some superficial or sensual quality. Those who make friends for the sake of profit in business are only apparent friends, their friendship being based not on love for one other but on desire for profit. The following two maxims are two strong pillars to support the Christian life, the first, *Those who fear God will come by true friendship*,[1] the second, *The world's friendship means enmity with God*.[2]

23. MORTIFICATION

It is said that if we write some word on an almond that is sound, replace the shell, and plant it, all its fruit will bear this word. I myself, Philothea, have never approved the method of those who, to reform a man, begin with exterior things such as deportment, clothing or hair. On the contrary, it seems to me that we must begin with the heart. *Turn the whole bent of your hearts back to me*,[3] says the Lord; and, *My son, give me the gifs of thy heart*;[4] for our actions take on the quality of the heart from which they proceed. The divine Spouse in the Canticles says to the soul: *Hold me close to thy heart, close as locket or bracelet fits*,[5] and it is certain that whoever has Christ in his heart soon has him in all that he does. That is why, Philothea, I have desired above all to impress the Holy Name of Jesus on your heart, confident that, from then on, all that comes from your heart, as the almond tree from the nut, will be stamped with this name, and that as Jesus lives in your heart so also he will live in your every act, will be seen in your eyes, your mouth and hands; with all your heart and in all reverence you will be able to say with St Paul : *I am alive, or rather, not I; it is Christ that lives in me*.[6] To put it briefly, to gain the heart is to gain

[1] Ecclus. 6. 17.   [2] James 4. 4.   [3] Joel 2. 12.   [4] Prov. 23.26.
[5] Cant. 8.6.   [6] Gal. 2. 20.

the whole man; nevertheless the heart must be taught how to direct its outward actions that they may manifest not only devotion but also great wisdom and discretion. Consequently I will give you some brief counsels: If you are able to fast you would do well to fast a little more often than the Church demands, for besides elevating the spirit, subduing the flesh, practising virtue and acquiring greater merit, this serves to maintain our mastery over greediness and to subject our bodily appetites to the law of the spirit; and even though we do not fast very much nevertheless the devil fears us more when he sees that we are able to fast. Wednesdays, Fridays, and Saturdays are the days on which the early Christians most often practised abstinence, so you may choose some of these days as fast days, in the measure of your devotion, and according to your confessor's advice.

I would willingly say, as St Jerome said to the devout Laeta, "I am very displeased by long immoderate fasts, especially in the case of the young, having learnt by experience that the little donkey tries to turn aside from the path when tired," in other words, young people who have harmed their health by excessive fasting turn only too easily to dainty food. Stags run badly both when they are too fat and when they are too lean; to weaken our body exposes us to temptation as much as to pamper it; too much comfort making the body insolent, too much discomfort making it desperate; and as we cannot carry it when it is too fat, so it cannot carry us when it is too thin. Such want of moderation in fasting, taking the discipline, wearing a hair shirt and so on, renders the best years of many people useless in the service of charity, as happened in the case of St Bernard, who regretted his excessive austerities, for having ill treated their body in the beginning they are often forced to pamper it in the end. They would have done much better had they treated it reasonably in a way compatible with their duties and state of life. The flesh is subdued both by fasting and by work; if your work is necessary and useful to God's glory I would rather you suffered the labour than the fasting, as more in accordance with the mind of the Church, for our duty to God and our neighbour dispenses us even from fasts of obligation. One has the hardship of fasting, the other of serving the sick, visiting those in prison, hearing confessions, preaching, helping those in need, praying and so on; all of which are more valuable than fasting, for they not only subdue the body, but also bear excellent fruit. In general, it is better to over-strengthen than over-weaken our body; we can always curb it when necessary, we cannot always restore it when we want to.

We should always remember our lord's words to his disciples : *Be content to eat the fare they offer you.*[1] In my opinion to eat whatever is set before us, as and when it is set before us, whether we like it or not, is more virtuous than always to choose the worst; the latter may seem more austere yet it lacks that resignation by which we not only give up our own *taste* but also our own choice. There is no little austerity in always accommodating our taste to whatever is put before us; such mortification makes no show, causes no inconvenience and is very suitable for those who live in the world. To refuse one dish for the sake of another, to sample everything, find nothing well cooked, or properly clean, and to make mysteries of every mouthful, indicates a pampered heart which can

[1] Luke 10.8.

rise no higher than plates and dishes. I consider St Bernard more virtuous when he drank oil in mistake for water or wine, than if he had drunk wormwood on purpose, for it showed his indifference to what he was drinking.

The perfect practice of the maxim, *Be content to eat the fare they offer you*, consists in such indifference. This does not apply, of course, to food which might harm one's health or not agree with us because too highly seasoned, rich, or flatulent; nor does it apply if we need nourishment and strength to do our work for God. Consistent moderation is better than occasional immoderate abstinence followed by indulgence. The discipline is an excellent means of stimulating our devotion if used with moderation and the hair shirt an excellent means of subduing the flesh, though normally unsuitable for those who are married, have delicate constitutions, or are engaged in any difficult work; on special days of penance, however, it may be used subject to our confessor's advice.

Every night we should take the sleep we need to keep usefully awake the next day for there is great virtue in going to bed early that we may rise early; countless examples in the scriptures and in the lives of the saints, and natural reasons also, point to the morning as the best and most fruitful part of the day; remember, our Lord is called *The Rising Sun*[1] and our Lady *The Dawn of Day*.[1] Certainly dawn is the most beautiful, the most pleasant and the most peaceful time of day, the very birds inviting us to rise and praise God, so that early rising is conducive both to health and holiness.

Balaam on his ass went in search of Balac, but, since

[1] Zach. 3. 8. 2 Cant. 6.9.

his intention was not right, an angel with a sword stood in his way to slay him. The ass, seeing the angel, twice turned aside from the path as though from stubbornness while Balaam beat her cruelly with his staff to make her go forward, until the third time, *she lay down under her rider; so that Balaam fell into a rage and beat her flanks harder than ever. Hereupon the Lord endowed the ass with the power of speech, and she said, This is the third time thou hast beaten me; what have I done to deserve it? . . . Then the Lord opened Balaam's eyes, to make him see the angel . . . If the ass had not turned aside, said the angel, I would have taken thy life. I have been at fault, said Balaam, little thinking that thou wert standing in my way.*[1] Notice, Philothea, Balaam was at fault yet he struck the innocent ass.

How often, for example, will a woman whose husband or child falls ill begin at once to fast, wear a hair shirt, and take the discipline, in imitation of David on a similar occasion! Why beat the poor ass, your body, which cannot help you and is not the cause of God's sword being drawn against you? Rather correct your heart which idolizes your husband, and pampers the child in countless ways, paving the way for pride, vanity and ambition. A man, full of remorse for sins of the flesh, goes to meet his conscience, sword in hand, to pierce it with holy fear; at once his heart is awakened and cries out, "O evil flesh, treacherous body, you have betrayed me", then he attacks his flesh ruthlessly with immoderate fasting, excessive use of the discipline and an insupportable hair shirt. The flesh, if it could speak to the soul as the ass to Balaam, would say, "Why do you strike me? It is against *you* that God's vengeance

[1] Num. 22. 21-34.

is directed; *you* are the criminal. Why do you lead me into bad company? Why abuse my eyes and hands and lips? Why trouble me with evil thoughts? Have good thoughts and I will not be moved to evil; mix with those who are modest and my passions will not be aroused. You cast me into the fire, and do not expect me to burn; cast smoke in my eyes and expect them to see clearly." It is certain that God, on such occasions, says to you: *It is your hearts that must be torn asunder*,[1] for it is principally against them that his wrath is kindled. To wash and bathe ourselves is not so sure a cure for the itch as to purify the blood and cleanse the liver; so, to cure ourselves of sinful habits, it is certainly useful to mortify the flesh, but much more necessary to purify and cleanse our heart. In any case, we should never undertake corporal austerities without our confessor's advice.

24. SOCIETY AND SOLITUDE

To go to extremes in seeking and in shunning company are equally blameworthy for those who live in the world. The former is a sign of idleness and laziness, the latter indicates disdain or contempt for those about us. You should love your neighbour as yourself; to show that you love him you must not avoid his company, and to show also that you love yourself you must be content with your own company when alone. "Think first of yourself," says St Bernard, "then of others." If there is no good reason for seeking the company of others or for entertaining them at home, keep yourself company; but if others come to you, Philothea, or if there is good

[1] Joel 2.13.

reason to seek them, mix with them willingly and cheerfully, in God's name.

That company is bad, which is assembled for some evil intention or when the persons themselves are evil, indiscreet and dissolute; you must avoid such company as bees avoid wasps and hornets.

The sweat, breath and saliva of those who have been bitten by a mad dog are infectious particularly with regard to children and delicate persons. In the same way we cannot mix with those who are vicious and dissolute without danger, especially if our devotion is still tender and delicate. Some social gatherings have no other end but recreation, and are merely a diversion from serious occupation: as far as these are concerned, we should not be too attached to them nor devote to them more than our spare time. Some visits are necessary out of politeness, for example, social calls to pay our respects to our neighbours; in such cases we should neither be too punctilious in their fulfilment nor so impolite as to neglect them, but fulfil our obligations, modestly avoiding bad manners on the one hand and frivolity on the other. Lastly, there are those occasions when we associate with good and virtuous people and these are most profitable, Philothea; for as a vine planted among olive trees bears luscious grapes flavoured with olive, so those who mix with virtuous people cannot but acquire their qualities.

Alone, drones cannot make honey, but they can with the help of the bees ; in the same way with the help of those who are devout we can more easily practise devotion. In no matter what company, always be candid and simple, gentle and modest. Some people are incapable of behaving without so much affectation that they irritate everyone. Those who are always affected, who watch themselves in all they do, are as annoying as if they could never walk without counting every step nor say anything without singing; such behaviour merely indicates conceit. In company we should always be cheerful; St Romuald and St Antony are highly praised because, in spite of all their austerities they were always joyful, gay and courteous in all they said and did; as St Paul says: *Rejoice with them that rejoice,*[1] but *rejoice in the Lord,* and *let your modesty be known to all men.*[2]

To *rejoice in the Lord* means that your joy must arise from something both lawful and becoming, for not all that is lawful is becoming; *to let your modesty be known* means that you must refrain from any bad behaviour, avoiding for example such foolish and unkind jokes as tripping people up, dirtying their face, sticking a pin in them, or mocking a half-wit.

Over and above that spiritual retirement which you can practise in the midst of even important affairs, have a love for true solitude, not to the extent of going into the desert like St Mary of Egypt, St Paul, St Antony, and the other fathers of the desert, but by spending some time alone, in your room, garden or anywhere else where you can the more easily enter into your soul. Then refresh yourself with some spiritual reading or with good and holy thoughts, following the example of that great Bishop, Gregory Nazianzen, who says: "I used to walk by myself at sunset and wander on the sea shore; such recreation would refresh me and help me to shake off some of my everyday troubles." He then goes on to tell us something of his thoughts, as I have already mentioned. Or follow the example of St Ambrose; St Augustine says that often, when he entered his room which was open to

[1] Rom. 12. 15.   [2] Phil. 4. 4-5.

all, he found him reading, and after waiting a while he
would go away without saying a word for fear of disturb-
ing him, not wishing to deprive this great pastor of what
little time he had to refresh his soul after the worry of his
various affairs. Our Lord himself said to the Apostles,
when they came to him and told him of their preaching
and of how much they had done, *Come away into a quiet
place by yourselves, and rest a little.*[1]

25. PROPER ATTIRE

ST PAUL wishes devout women (and men also) *to dress
themselves modestly and with restraint in befitting attire.*[2]
The decency of apparel and other ornaments depends on
the material, the style and on cleanliness. All our clothes
should be clean and we should as far as possible never
allow any stains or dirt to remain on them. Outward
cleanliness reflects to some extent cleanliness of soul.
God himself demands bodily cleanliness in those who
approach the altar and minister to souls. With regard to
the material and the style of our clothes, decency is determined largely by circumstances of time, age, state of
life, company and occasion. We normally dress better
on feast days, according to their importance; in time
of penance such as Lent, we put our bright clothes aside;
at weddings we wear wedding garments; at funerals
mourning; at Court we wear state attire and take it off
when we go home. A married woman may make herself attractive to please her husband when she is with
him, but if she does so when she is away from him,
people wonder for whose particular benefit she does so.
Young women may wear more attractive clothes for they

[1] Mark 6. 31.   [2] 1 Tim. 2. 9.

may lawfully seek to pleasure those among whom they hope to win a husband; nor is there any harm in marriageable widows wearing attractive clothes, so long as they do not appear frivolous; having been mothers of a family and having passed through the sorrow of widowhood, they are expected to be more mature and serious minded; for those who are widows in heart also, humility, modesty and devotion are their best adornments, for they cease to be true widows if they wish to win the love of men, and if such is not their wish, why should they dress as though it were? He who does not wish for lodgers should take down the sign outside his house. We laugh at the aged who seek to pass as beautiful, a foolishness tolerated only in the young.

Always be neat, Philothea; never wear untidy or badly fitting clothes; to be badly dressed shows a contempt for those with whom you live. On the other hand, guard against affectation, vanity, singularity and frivolity; always prefer simplicity and modesty, which are certainly beauty's best adornment and the best apology for plainness. St Peter warns young women in particular not to wear extravagant hair styles;[1] men who go in for such vanity are always considered effeminate, whilst vanity in young women indicates a weakness in their chastity. They say that they mean no harm, but the devil certainly does; for my part I would have the devout man or woman the best dressed in the company, but with the least show and affectation, adorned with his or her own graciousness, dignity and good repute. St Louis says that "everyone should dress according to his state in life, so that the wise and good cannot say you do too much, nor young persons say you do too little"; but should the

[1] 1 Pet. 3. 3.

young be dissatisfied with what is proper they must abide by the counsel of the wise.

26. HOW TO SPEAK OF GOD

DOCTORS diagnose a man's state of health by looking at his tongue; and our words are true indications of the state of our soul: *Thy words*, says our Lord, *will be matter to acquit, or matter to condemn thee.*[1]

We readily place our hand on the pain we feel and our tongue turns as readily to speak of what we love. If you truly love God, Philothea, you will often speak of him in conversation with your family, your friends, and neighbours, for *right reason is on the good man's lips, well weighed are all his counsels.*[2] As the mouth of the bee is only used for honey, so should your tongue be ever honeyed, as it were, with God, while you are never more happy than when you have his praises on your lips.

It is said of St Francis that he used to lick his lips after pronouncing the name of God, as though he found there the greatest sweetness in the world. But always speak of God as of God; in other words, with reverence and devotion, with love and humility, not ostentatiously playing the master. Let fall, as far as possible, the delicious honey of devotion, drop by drop, now in the ear of one, now in the ear of another; praying secretly in your soul that God may let it sink into their hearts. Above all do this with gentleness and kindness; not as though correcting them, but by inspiring them; for it is wonderful how powerfully hearts are moved when goodness is set before them in a fair and lovely guise. Never speak of God or of devotion without thinking, nor merely for the sake of talking, but always with attention and reverence.

[1] Matt..12. 37.   [2] Ps. 36. 30.

I said this to put you on your guard against that form of vanity found in many who profess devotion, who say holy and pious things as a matter of course on every possible occasion without ever thinking what they say, and then imagine they are as holy as their words indicate.

27. RESPECT IN CONVERSATION

A MAN *who is not betrayed into faults of the tongue,* says St James, *must be a man perfect at every point.*[1] Be very careful never to say anything unseemly, for though your intention may be good your hearers may take it otherwise. An improper word falling into a weak heart extends and spreads like a drop of oil on cloth, sometimes obsessing the heart and filling it with countless bad thoughts and temptations. As the body is poisoned through the mouth, so is the heart poisoned through the ears, making the person who speaks such words a murderer. For even though it may happen that the poison does not take effect, the heart of the hearer being strengthened by some antidote, this is not due to any lack of malice on the part of the speaker. There is no point in saying that he intended no evil, for our Lord, who knows our thoughts, has said, *It is from the heart's overflow that the mouth speaks,*[2] and though we may not intend the evil the devil does, and he always uses such words secretly to wound someone's heart. It is said that the breath of those who have eaten the herb called *angelica* is always sweet and agreeable; so the words of those who have chastity and modesty in their heart are always agreeable, pure and modest. As for anything obscene or indecent, St Paul will not have it *to be*

[1] James 3. 2.   [2] Matt. 12. 34.

as much as named,[1] assuring us that nothing so corrupts noble minds as bad company.[2] Such words spoken with ambiguity and subtly and with guile are more poisonous than ever; the sharper the dart the more easily it enters our body, so the more pointed and evil the remark the more deeply it enters the heart. Those who imagine that such words show them to be men of the world are ignorant of the purpose of conversation, for they should be like bees gathered together to draw honey from some delightful and virtuous conversation, not like a swarm of wasps feeding on garbage. If some fool speaks indecently to you, show that you are offended by turning away or by any other means your prudence may suggest. Mockery is one of the worst of vices, one which God detests and one which he has often punished in strange ways in the past. Nothing is so opposed to charity, and even more to devotion, as contempt and scorn for those about us. Derision or mockery always involves contempt and so is gravely sinful, so that theologians rightly hold mockery for the worst sin of the tongue we can commit against our neighbour; for other offences are committed with some respect for the person offended, but this is committed with contempt and scorn. But with regard to what we say in fun and with innocent humour, this pertains to the virtue which the Greeks called *eutrapelia*, and which we may refer to as gaiety, by means of which we derive friendly amusement from the humorous situations which arise from human imperfection; but we must be very careful lest this degenerate into mockery. Mockery provokes laughter out of scorn and contempt for our neighbour, but innocent humour and friendly laughter at some witty

[1] Eph. 5. 3.   [2] Cf. 1 Cor. 15. 33.

saying, arises from a lawful freedom and familiarity.

When devout persons wished to speak to St Louis of serious matters after dinner, he used to say: "This is not the time to engage in learned discussions but to relax with wit and humour"; thus putting at their ease the nobles gathered round him to receive his favours. But, Philothea, let us so pass the time by recreation that we may gain eternity by devotion.

28. RASH JUDGEMENT

JUDGE *nobody, and you will not be judged*; says our Saviour, *condemn nobody, and you will not be condemned.*[1] St Paul says, *You do ill to pass judgement prematurely, before the Lord's coming; he will bring to light what is hidden in darkness, and reveal the secrets of men's hearts.*[2]

The judgements of men are always rash because they are not judges of one another, and in judging they merely usurp the office of our Lord. They are rash because the malice of sin depends primarily on the intention which is kept secret in men's hearts, and as far as we are concerned is *hidden in darkness*; they are rash because we have enough to do to judge ourselves without trying to judge others. To avoid being judged ourselves it is as necessary that we avoid judging others as that we judge ourselves; the first being forbidden by our Lord, the second commanded by St Paul who says, *If we would judge ourselves we would not be judged.*[3] But we do just the opposite, for we always do what is forbidden, judging those about us on every possible occasion, and never do what we are commanded, namely, judge ourselves. The remedy for rash judgement is to be sought in the causes from which it springs.

1 Luke 6. 37.   2 1 Cor. 4. 5.   3 1 Cor. 11. 31.

Some hearts, naturally sour, bitter and harsh, embitter and make sour everything they receive and, in the words of Amos, *poison the springs of right and justice*,[1] ever judging their neighbour rigorously and harshly; such people need to fall into the hands of a good spiritual physician, for this bitterness, being natural to them, is very hard to overcome, and though it is rather an imperfection than a sin, it is nevertheless dangerous, for it opens the soul to rash judgement and slander, and gives them full rein. Some judge rashly from pride rather than hardness of heart, imagining that they increase their honour in the measure in which they lower that of others. They are ignorant, presumptuous and so full of their own esteem that they look down on everybody else; "*I am not like the rest of men*",[2] said the foolish Pharisee. Others are not so openly proud but only take a certain pleasure in considering the imperfections of others, that they may indulge in self-satisfaction and cause others to admire the contrary perfection which they imagine they possess; but this is something so hidden and subtle that they are unlikely to recognize it unless it is pointed out to them. Others, to justify their conduct to their own conscience, are only too ready to judge others guilty of their own vices, imagining that there is safety in numbers. Many indulge in rash judgements simply because they enjoy philosophizing and speculating about the morals and dispositions of others, more as an intellectual exercise than anything else; and if, unfortunately, they happen to be right, their rashness and the desire to go on increase, with little hope of remedy. Others judge according to their feelings, thinking well of those they

[1] Amos 6. 13.   [2] Luke 18. 11.

love and ill of those they dislike, except in the extraordinary yet only too real case when excess of love leads them to judge ill of the one they love; but such a monstrous effect proceeds only from a love which is impure, imperfect, disordered and unhealthy, and this is jealousy, which, as everyone knows, for a mere look, the most fleeting smile, will convict a person of adultery and unfaithfulness.

Fear and ambition, and other similar weaknesses of character, often give rise to suspicion and rash judgement. What is the remedy? Those who drink the juice of an Ethiopian herb called *ophiusa* see imaginary serpents and others horrors everywhere. So those who have imbibed pride, envy, ambition and hatred see guilt and evil everywhere. The antidote for *ophiusa* is palm oil; in the latter case I recommend that they drink as much of the sacred wine of charity as possible, for it will free them from the evil dispositions which cause them to make such evil judgements.

Those who are charitable never look for evil but rather fear to meet it, and when they do meet it they turn away as though they had not done so; they even close their eyes at the very whisper of it, believing with holy simplicity that it was only the shadow or appearance of evil. If they cannot help recognizing the evil they turn away at once and try to forget all about it. Charity is the best remedy for all evils but for this especially. Everything seems yellow to those who have jaundice and it is said that the cure is to place celandine under the soles of the feet. Those who suffer from spiritual jaundice, in other words rash judgement, see evil everywhere. To be cured they must apply the remedy, not to their eyes or understanding, but to their dispositions, which are, as it were, the feet of the soul; for when these are well ordered and charitable so will be their judgements. I will give you three good examples: Isaac had said that Rebecca was his sister: Abimelech saw him caress her tenderly and therefore judged her to be his wife; an evil-minded person would rather have judged her to be a harlot, or, if she were his sister, incestuous. Abimelech put the most charitable construction he could on what he saw, and we must always do the same, Philothea, judging our neighbour favourably as far as we can; were there a hundred different ways of looking on an action, we should choose the most favourable one.

St Joseph saw quite clearly that our Lady was with child, but on the other hand seeing her holiness and angelic purity, he could never believe that this had come about unlawfully and so resolved to let God be the judge. Though there was strong enough evidence for judging her unfavourably he would pass no judgement at all; and why was this? Because, says the Holy Spirit, *he was a right-minded man,*[1] and the right-minded man, when he can no longer excuse the deed or the intention of someone he knows to be good, leaves it to God. Our Crucified Saviour, unable to excuse the sin of those who crucified him, minimized their malice by pleading their ignorance. So if we cannot excuse a sin, let us at least be compassionate, attributing it to such extenuating causes as ignorance or weakness. May we then never judge our neighbour? No, Philothea, never; even in a court of justice, it is God who is th ejudge; true, he makes uses of magistrates that his judgements may be heard, but they are only his spokesmen and interpreters and as

[1] Matt. 1. 19.

such should pronounce only that judgement they have learnt from him. If they act otherwise, following their own feelings, then it is they alone who judge and who in consequence are judged, for it is forbidden for men, as such, to judge others. To see or know something is not to judge it; for judgement, in the sense used in the Scriptures, presupposes some difficulty great or small, true or apparent, which must be resolved; that is why we read: *The man who does not believe is already judged*;[1] there is no need of judgement for there is no doubt of their damnation. This does not mean we may not *doubt* our neighbour; we are not forbidden to doubt, only forbidden to judge, nevertheless, we may only doubt and suspect others in so far as we have good reason and evidence for doing so, otherwise our doubts and suspicions are rash. Had some evil-minded person seen Jacob kiss Rachel at the well, or Rebecca accept bracelets and earrings from Eliezer, who was a stranger there, they would no doubt have thought ill of these two models of chastity, but without reason or cause, for it is rash to draw a bad conclusion from an indifferent action unless other circumstances move us to do so. It is also rash to blame a person on the evidence of a single act, but I will say more of this later.

To conclude, those who keep a careful guard on their conscience rarely make rash judgements; as bees in misty or cloudy weather retire to the hive and concern themselves with the honey, so the thoughts of the virtuous are restrained from inquiry into hidden matters or the obscure actions of those about them, and instead are concerned with good resolutions for their own amendment; to concern ourselves with examining the lives of others betokens a futile mind. This does not apply to those who

[1] Jojn 3. 18.

have charge of others in a family, or community, for their duty largely consists in keeping watch and guard over the conduct of others; they should do their duty lovingly, and then mind their own business.

29. DETRACTION

RASH judgement gives rise to disquiet, contempt of those about us, pride, self-complacency and hundreds of other evil effects, the worst of which is detraction, the greatest bane of society. If only I had one of the burning coals from the holy altar with which to touch the lips of men, as the seraph purified the lips of Isaias[1], that their guilt might be swept away and their sins pardoned! To rid the world of detraction would be to rid it of most of its iniquity. To take away one neighbour's good name unjustly is a sin and we are bound to make reparation, depending on the nature of the detraction; no one can enter heaven with another's goods and the best of all exterior goods is our good name.

Detraction is a kind of murder. We have three lives: our spiritual life, depending on the grace of God, our bodily life, depending upon the soul, and our social life, depending on our good name; sin destroys the first, death the second, detraction the third. Anyone who commits the sin of detraction usually commits three murders with a single stroke of his tongue: the spiritual murder of his own soul, and of the soul of anyone who listens to him, while destroying the social life of the one he defames. St Bernard says: "He who defames and he who listens are possessed by the devil. One has him on his tongue, the other in his ear," while

[1] Cf. Isa. 6. 6.

David says of detractors that *their tongues are sharp as the tongues of serpents.*[1] Like the serpent's tongue, the tongue of the detractor is forked; it has to strike but once to sting and poison the ears of those who listen and the reputation of those he speaks against. I beg you, then, Philothea, never to defame anyone directly or indirectly; take care never to impute evils, crimes and sins to those about you, or make known those that are secret, or exaggerate those that are known; never put a bad construction on what is good in itself nor deny the good you know a person to possess; never ignore this good out of malice, nor diminish it by words, for in all these ways you would greatly offend God, especially by false accusations and by denying the truth on which your neighbour's good name depends, for in a single act you commit a double sin: by lying and by injuring your neighbour.

Those who preface their detraction with favourable remarks or mingle what they say with compliments and pleasantries are the most subtle and pernicious of all. "Of course I am very fond of him", they say, "and in every other way he is very honourable, but the truth must be told and such a breach of faith is very wrong." "She is a very good girl of course; she was simply taken by surprise", and so on. The artifice is obvious. As an archer draws the arrow to himself as closely as possible to shoot it with all the greater force, so such detractors seem to draw their words to themselves, but only to discharge them with greater force and drive them more deeply into the hearts of their hearers.

Witty detraction is the cruellest of all. Hemlock when taken alone is a fairly slow and harmless poison and

[1] Ps. 139. 4.

168

easily cured, but it is incurable when taken with wine, so a slander which would normally go in one ear and out of the other sticks in the mind when given a clever and amusing guise. The lips of such detractors, says David, *hide the poison of asps.*[1] The sting of the asp is almost imperceptible and its poison first stimulates the heart and stomach to make them more receptive, after which there is no cure.

Never call a person a drunkard because you have once seen him drunk, nor say he is incestuous or adulterous because he was once caught in the act, for he is not made such by a single act.

The sun once stood still that Josue might win a battle, and it was once darkened at the death of our Lord, yet this does not make us say that it is either immovable or dark.

Noe was once drunk and so was Lot, who was also guilty of an act of incest, yet this does not mean that they were drunkards nor that Lot was incestuous; St Peter once shed blood, but this does not mean he was bloodthirsty, nor was he a blasphemer because he once blasphemed. To be credited with a vice or virtue the action must be protracted and habitual. So it would be untrue to call a man bad-tempered or a thief because he was once angry or once guilty of stealing.

We may still be wrong in calling a man evil though he may have been such for a long time. Simon the Leper called Magdalen a sinner because this had recently been the case, but he was wrong because instead of being a sinner now she was a holy penitent and that is why our Lord defended her.

The foolish Pharisee considered the publican a

[1] Ps. 139. 4.

sinner, perhaps a thief, a cheat or an adulterer, but he was greatly mistaken, for the publican was at that time high in God's favour.[1]

Since, through the goodness of God, we may ask and receive his grace in a moment, how can we be sure that the sinner of yesterday is still a sinner today? We must not judge yesterday by today, nor today by yesterday. On the last day alone is judgement irrevocable. We can never call a man wicked without danger of error, only say, if it is necessary to say anything, that he once did something evil or lived an evil life for some particular time, perhaps that he is doing evil now, for we cannot argue from the present to the past or the past to the present, and still less to the future.

Though we must take great care not to destroy our neighbour's good name, we must avoid the opposite extreme of which some are guilty who, to avoid detraction, praise and speak well of vices. Do not excuse someone guilty of detraction by saying he is frank and outspoken; nor call someone who is conceited and affected large minded and cultivated. Do not refer to dangerous familiarities as innocent and harmless liberties nor clothe disobedience in the guise of zeal, call arrogance sincerity, or flirtation merely friendship. No, Philothea, we must never, on the pretext of avoiding detraction, praise, tolerate or encourage any of the other vices, but rather frankly and openly condemn evil, and blame what is blameworthy; by so doing we give glory to God, so long as we fulfil the following conditions. To be justified in blaming the vices of others, it must be necessary for the good of those we blame or of those to whom we speak. Say, for example, that I hear someone

[1] Cf. Luke 18. 11, 14.

discussing in the presence of young girls the dangerous familiarities of certain men and women; they will listen and be led astray if I excuse such behaviour or do not openly condemn it; for their sake I must do so frankly at the time, unless I can do it later with more effect and less harm to the persons concerned. It is also necessary that it should be my duty to speak as, for example, the most prominent person in the company, when my silence would seem to give consent; otherwise I should not take this task upon myself.

Above all I must choose my words very carefully and not say too much; for example, if I blame some familiarity between a young man and a young woman because it seems indiscreet and dangerous I must not exaggerate in the slightest; if there is only a suspicion of indiscretion I will say no more than that. If it is merely an indiscretion I will not speak of it as worse. If there is neither indiscretion nor grounds for reasonable suspicion but only what furnishes a pretext for an evil-minded detractor, I will say simply that or nothing at all. While I speak of a neighbour, my tongue is like a lancet in the hands of a surgeon who wishes to make an incision between nerve and sinew; it must be equally accurate, speaking the precise truth. Lastly, and above all, take care, when condemning a sin, to spare the sinner as much as you can. We may, it is true, speak freely of infamous and notorious public sinners so long as we do so in a spirit of charity and mercy, avoiding arrogance and presumption and not taking pleasure in their misfortune, for this would mark us as mean and base. This does not apply, of course, to those who are openly enemies of God and of his Church, for we must denounce heretics, schismatics and their leaders to the best of our ability, charity bidding us cry wolf when the flock is in danger.

Everyone takes it upon himself to judge and criticize rulers and other nations according to the way he feels about them. Never fall into this fault, Philothea, for besides offending God it will only involve you in endless disputes.

When you hear anyone defamed, throw doubt upon the accusation, if you can justly do so; if not, credit the person accused with good intentions. If that fails, show compassion for him and change the subject, reminding yourself and those present that they who do not fall owe it entirely to God. Rebuke the detractor gently and say what good you know of the person defamed.

30. FURTHER ADVICE ON CONVERSATION

ALWAYS speak openly, frankly, sincerely, gently and honestly, avoiding duplicity, pretence and dissimulation; for though it is not always a good thing to speak the whole truth yet it is never lawful to say anything untrue. Make a habit of never telling a lie, either to excuse yourself, or for any other reason, remembering that God is *the God of truth*.[1] If you do tell a lie inadvertently, correct it at once, if you can; by doing so you will more than compensate for the lie itself. Though we may sometimes, discreetly and prudently, disguise or hide the truth by some equivocation, we should only do so in a matter of importance when the service and glory of God obviously demands it: in any other case it is dangerous, for, as it says in the Scriptures, *the holy spirit will not abide in a deceitful soul*.[2] Simplicity is the

[1] Ps. 30. 6.   [2] Wisd. 1. 5.

best and most desirable artifice; worldly wisdom and human artifice belong to the children of the world, but the children of God are straightforward in their dealings and their heart is free from guile. *He walks secure,* says Solomon, *who walks sincerely.*[1] Lying, duplicity and dissimulation are always the mark of a weak and ignoble spirit.

When St Augustine first wrote his *Confessions* he said, in Book Four, that he and his friend had but one soul and that when his friend died he had a horror of living, not wishing to live by halves, yet a horror also of dying lest his friend should die altogether. In the book of his *Retractions* he took back these words as being foolish, artificial and affected, so you see, Philothea, how sensitive he was with regard to any affectation in words.

Frankness, candour and sincerity in speech enhance the beauty of the Christian life. *It was my resolve to live watchfully,* said David, *and never use my tongue amiss.*[2] *Set a guard, O Lord, on my mouth, a barrier to fence in my lips.*[3] St Louis used to say that, to avoid all argument and quarrelling, we should never contradict anyone, unless to agree with him would be sinful and harmful. When it is necessary to contradict anyone or to defend our own opinion against his, we should do so tactfully and gently without trying to brow-beat him, for we gain nothing by being boorish. The advice of the wise men of old, that we should speak little, does not mean that we should speak few words, but that we should not speak many idle words, for it is a matter of quality rather than of quantity. To my mind we should avoid both extremes, for to be too strictly reserved, refusing to take part in any conversation, would indicate either

[1] Prov. 10. 9.   [2] Ps.38 1.   [3] Ps. 140. 3.

173

want of confidence or contempt; while on the other
hand to be always talking and chattering, without giving
anyone else a chance to speak, is a sign of superficiality
and frivolity. St Louis did not like people to carry on
private and confidential conversations with one another
in company and particularly at table, lest others fear
they were being talked about. He used to say: "If
anyone at table in good company has something
amusing and pleasing to say he should say it so that
everyone can hear; if it concerns a serious matter let him
keep it for another time."

31. LAWFUL RECREATIONS

SOME recreation is necessary to refresh mind and body.
Cassian tells us that a hunter once found St John the
Evangelist holding a partridge in his hand and amusing
himself by stroking it. When the hunter asked him how
so great a man could waste his time in such a trivial way
St John replied: "Why do you not carry your bow always
taut?" "Because", replied the hunter, "it would then
lose its resilience, and so be rendered useless." "Do not
be surprised then," said the Apostle, "if I sometimes
relax my mind and take a little recreation so that afterwards I may concentrate the better." It is certainly
wrong to be so strict with oneself, so austere and un-
sociable, as to deny oneself, and everyone else, recreation. To go out in the fresh air, to go for a walk,
to take part in cheerful and friendly conversation, to
sing or play some musical instrument or other, or to go
hunting, are such innocent recreations that we may
always make good use of them so long as we exercise
that common prudence which governs time, place,

measure and order. Games in which success alone is the reward for skill and effort of mind or body, for example, tennis, ball, pall-mall, tilting, chess and backgammon are good and lawful so long as we guard against excess either in the time we spend on them or the stakes played for. To spend too much time on a game makes it an occupation rather than a recreation; instead of being refreshed we become tired and depressed! Five or six hours of chess would tire our minds as much as an excessively long game of tennis would exhaust our bodies. To play for extravagant stakes tends to make the players too excited, and in any case it is unreasonable to risk too much on the skill and effort required in such unimportant games. Above all, Philothea, take care that you never become attached to such things, for this would be wrong however good the recreation in itself. I do not mean that we should not enjoy such games, for they would then cease to be a recreation, but that we must never be so set on them that we desire them too eagerly or spend too much time on them.

32. UNDESIRABLE GAMES

GAMES of dice, cards and so on in which success depends largely on chance are not only dangerous recreations like dances, but are evil and reprehensible in themselves and so forbidden both by civil and ecclesiastical law. "What harm is there in such games?" you may say. It lies in the fact, Philothea, that success depends, not on reason, but on chance, which often favours those whose skill and effort are undeserving of victory, and this outrages reason. "But", you may say, "we all agree to this." That only proves that the

winner does not wrong the others, it does not prove that
you were reasonable to agree, nor does it make the
games reasonable, for success should be the reward of
skill not of chance, to which no merit attaches. Such
games are supposed to be recreation yet they are rather
absorbing occupations demanding continual attention
and concentration and involving endless worry and
anxiety. There is no concentration so morose, gloomy
and depressing as that of gamblers; no one may speak
or laugh, or even cough, while they are playing for fear
of annoying them. In fact there is no joy in gambling
at all, except in the case of the winner, whose joy is
reprehensible since it depends on the loss and misery
of the losers. When St Louis on his sick bed heard that
his brother, the Count of Anjou, and Monsieur Gautier
de Nemours were gambling, he got up and staggered
to their room, took hold of the tables, the dice and the
money and in his anger threw them out of the window
into the sea.

The devout Sarah, pleading her innocence before
God, said: *Thou, Lord, can bear me witness that I never
cast in my lot with the lovers of dalliance.*[1]

33. DANGEROUS PASTIMES

BALLS and dances are neither good nor evil in themselves but the way they are usually conducted tends to
evil and so makes them dangerous. Taking place at
night the darkness and soft lights provide ample opportunity for over-familiarity in the case of those who
are susceptible. They last half the night so that the next
morning is lost, as far as the service of God is concern-

[1] Tob. 3. 16, 17.

ed. It is, in any case, always foolish to turn day into night, light into darkness, and to exchange useless occupations for good ones. At a ball everyone tries to surpass everyone else in vanity, which only too easily encourages evil desires and moral laxity.

Dances are like pumpkins and mushrooms, Philothea, the best of which, according to doctors, are good for nothing. If you must eat pumpkins, however, make sure they are well prepared; in other words if you cannot avoid attending some dance make sure that you dance with modesty, dignity and with a good intention. According to doctors we should only eat mushrooms occasionally and then only sparingly, for no matter how well prepared, too many would be bad for us. In the same way, Philothea, we should not go to too many dances or dance too much lest it becomes an obsession. Mushrooms, according to Pliny, because spongy and porous, easily absorb the poison of serpents or of anything infectious with which they come into contact. Dances, balls and all night parties usually absorb the vices and sins that reign there, such as quarrelling, envy, mockery and over-familiarity, and as such activities open the pores of the body, so they open the pores of the heart of those present, disposing it to be captured and poisoned the moment a serpent whispers impure suggestions, flatters or speaks frivolous words of love, or when some basilisk indulges in unchaste or wanton glances.

Such unsuitable recreations, Philothea, are nearly always dangerous; they dissipate our devotion, weaken our spiritual life, cool our charity, and leave our soul open to countless evils; they must therefore be used with great prudence. They say that after eating mushrooms we should drink good wine; so, after dances, you should counteract the dangerous impressions they may have left on your soul by some good and holy considerations, for example:

1. That while you were at the dance many souls were burning in hell for sins committed on such occasions.

2. That many religious and devout persons were at that time in the presence of God, singing his praises and contemplating his beauty; certainly spending their time much more profitably than you were.

3. That while you were dancing many people were dying in great pain, thousands were suffering on their sick beds, in hospitals or in the streets, from all sorts of diseases and fevers. They had no relief and you gave them no thought. Does it never occur to you that one day you may suffer as they do while others are dancing?

4. That our Lord, our Lady, the angels and the saints were looking down upon you there in pity at seeing your heart absorbed and occupied by such futile and trivial amusements.

5. That all the while time was slipping by and death was drawing nearer, mocking you and inviting you to his dance at which the music will be the mourning of your friends and where your only step will be from life to death; man's final dance in which he passes in a moment from time to an eternity of either suffering or happiness.

These are only a few considerations which I suggest; if you have a holy fear of God, he will suggest many others to the same effect.

34. WHEN SUCH AMUSEMENTS ARE LAWFUL

FOR such amusements to be lawful they should be sought for recreation, not merely because we are attached to them; we should indulge in them for a short time only, not until we are tired and worn out; and only occasionally or they will become, as I have said, an occupation. In what circumstances are they lawful? In the case of those which are indifferent there are many such circumstances; in the case of those which are forbidden, very few, for they are reprehensible and dangerous. If, with prudence and discretion, you do take part in them, to fall in with those in whose company you find yourself, simply fulfil the conditions I have laid down. Condescension, springing from charity, makes indifferent things good, dangerous things permissible and even minimizes the harm of those which are partly evil, so that games of chance, which otherwise would be reprehensible, are lawful if on occasion we take part in them out of charity. I was very pleased when I read in the life of St Charles Borromeo that he condescended to the Swiss in certain things concerning which he was usually very strict; and that St Ignatius Loyola accepted an invitation to play cards. St Elizabeth of Hungary used to play and dance sometimes at social gatherings without prejudicing her devotion which was so deeply rooted in her soul that, like the rocks about the lake of Rieti which grow when beaten by the waves, it grew amid the vanities and pleasures to which her state of life exposed her. Great fires are increased by the wind but little ones, if not well sheltered, are put out.

35. FIDELITY ON ALL OCCASIONS

THE sacred Spouse in the Canticle of Canticles says that his beloved has ravished his heart *with one glance of an eye, with one ringlet straying on her neck.*[1] Now of all the exterior parts of the body none is more noble either in the way it is made or in its action than the eye, and none of less account than the hair, and so the sacred Spouse indicates that he finds not only the great works of the devout acceptable, but also their very least, and that to please him we must be faithful in all things great or small since we can in either case ravish his heart by love.

Be prepared, then, Philothea, to undergo many great trials for his sake, even martyrdom; resolve, should he ask, to give him all you hold most dear: father, mother, brother, husband, wife, children, your eyes, your very life; such sacrifices must find your heart ready.

But as long as his Divine Providence spares you these great and painful trials, does not, for example, ask your eyes, at least give him your hair; in other words, bear patiently the small trials that are your daily lot, those little inconveniences and trifling losses which are so many opportunities for proving your love, winning his heart, and making it all your own. A headache, a toothache, or a cold; the bad temper of one's husband or wife; meeting with disdain or sulkiness; a glass broken; gloves, a ring or a handkerchief lost; the inconvenience of going to bed early or of rising early to pray or go to Communion; a feeling of embarrassment in performing certain devotions in public, all of these things, when accepted and embraced with love, are

[1] Cant. 4. 9.

most pleasing to God who for *a draught of cold water*[1] has promised his faithful a sea of perfect happiness, and as such opportunities occur every moment they enable us to heap up spiritual riches if only we take advantage of them. When I read about all the raptures and spiritual transports of St Catherine of Siena, of her wise counsels and conferences, I had no doubt that she had ravished the heart of her heavenly Spouse with the eyes of her soul; but I was equally impressed to find that she worked in her father's kitchen, humbly turned the spit, looked after the fire, cooked the food, kneaded the bread and carried out the most menial household tasks with a heart full of burning love for God; and I set no less store on the humble reflections she used to make while performing such lowly tasks than on the ecstasies and raptures she so often experienced, as a reward perhaps for her humility and abjection. She used to imagine, for example, when cooking her father's meals, that she was another Martha doing it for our Lord; she saw our Lady in her mother and the Apostles in her brothers, encouraging herself in this way to serve in spirit the heavenly court, and carrying out her menial tasks with great delight seeing them as the will of God. I give you this example, Philothea, to show you how important it is to direct our actions, however humble, to the service of God and advise you most earnestly to imitate the woman praised so highly by Solomon who put her hand to strong, noble and lofty things yet did not neglect her spinning wheel, *she hath put out her hand to strong things, and her fingers have taken hold of the spindle.*[2] Put your hand to strong things, Philothea, by prayer and meditation, by frequenting the sacraments

[1] Matt. 10.42.   [2] Prov. 31. 39.

and teaching others to love God, inspiring their hearts to good; in other words by doing all the great and important things whenever you have the opportunity. But do not forget your spinning wheel, that is to say, practise the humble and lowly virtues which grow, like flowers, at the foot of the cross: helping the poor, visiting the sick, looking after your family with all that this involves, above all practising that diligence which permits no idleness, all the while making use of such considerations as I have mentioned in the case of St Catherine. Great opportunities of serving God are rare, but little ones are frequent, and our Lord has told us that if we are *faithful over little things*, he will commit *great things* to our charge.[1] Do everything in God's name, then, and it will be done well; *whether you eat or drink*,[2] take recreation or turn the spit, you can profit in God's sight by doing them because it is his will.

36. WE MUST BE REASONABLE

WE are human beings because we have reason, yet it is rare to find anyone who is truly reasonable, for we are usually diverted from the path of reason by self-love which leads us to do countless little dangerous, unjust, and unfair things which like *the little foxes* spoken of in the Canticle of Canticles *destroy the vines*.[3] We think little of them because they are so small yet they do great damage by their very number. Are not the following things unjust and unreasonable? We condemn our neighbour for trifles yet make excuses for ourselves in important matters; we wish to sell very dear and buy very cheap; we want justice done in the case of others

[1] Cf. Matt. 25. 31.   [2] Col. 3. 17.   [3] Cant. 2. 15.

and claim mercy and indulgence in our own; we expect others to take our words in good part yet are touchy and over-sensitive ourselves. We are annoyed with our neighbour if he refuses to sell one of his possessions at the price we offer; though it is surely more reasonable that he should keep his property and let us keep our money; he should rather be annoyed with us for wishing to cause him inconvenience. If we are partial to some particular practice we despise all others and criticize those who do not think as we do. If we find one of our subordinates unpleasant or if we have conceived a dislike for him, he can do nothing right and we never cease persecuting and finding fault with him; while on the contrary, if we have taken a liking to someone there is nothing which we will not excuse. Some parents cannot tolerate an ugly child, no matter how good it may be, while they spoil a beautiful child even when it is badly behaved. We always prefer the rich to the poor even though they are not so noble or virtuous; we even prefer those who are best dressed. We are strict in exacting our own rights but expect others to be lenient in claiming theirs; we are punctilious in asserting our own position, but like to see others humble and condescending; we are quite prepared to complain of our neighbours, but they must never complain about us. We consider that we do a great deal for others but, of course, they do nothing for us. We are like the partridges of Paphlagonia which have two hearts, a gentle gracious and kindly heart for ourselves, a hard, strict, and severe heart for others. We have two weights; one for ourselves to our greatest advantage, another for our neighbour to his greatest disadvantage; as it says in the Scriptures: *None but exchanges empty forms of speech with his neighbour; everywhere false hearts and their treacherous lips;*[1] and to have two weights, *one weight for getting and one for giving, the Lord cannot endure.*[2] Be just and impartial in all you do, Philothea; always put yourself in your neighbour's place and him in yours, then your judgement will be fair. Put yourself in the place of the seller when you are buying, in the place of the buyer when you are selling, and you will buy and sell justly.

The injustices I have mentioned are of little account, not obliging us to restitution, for we do not exceed our strict rights in seeking our own advantage; but they oblige us to reform because they are faults against reason and charity; and, after all, we are only deceiving ourselves, for we lose nothing by being generous, noble and courteous or by having a loyal impartial and reasonable spirit. Remember, then, Philothea, to examine your heart often and see if you are treating your neighbour as you would wish him to treat you, were you in his place, for this is the proof of being truly reasonable. When Trajan was criticized by his friends for making himself too accessible he answered: "Should I not, as Emperor, behave towards my subjects as I would wish an Emperor to behave towards me if I were a subject?"

37. DESIRES

EVERYONE knows that we must never desire anything evil, such desire making us evil ourselves, but I say, Philothea, do not desire even dangerous things, such as the dances and games I have mentioned; do not

[1] Ps. 11. 3.   [2] Prov. 20. 23.

desire honours or high positions, or visions or ecstasies, for they open the way to danger, vanity and deception; do not desire what is far away or cannot happen for a long time, as many do, who merely tire and distract their hearts to no purpose and lay up a store of trouble. If a young man earnestly desires some post before he is ready for it, such a desire is useless; and what is the point of a married woman desiring to be a nun? If I desire to buy something that belongs to my neighbour before he is ready to sell it, such a desire is merely a waste of time. If a sick priest desires to preach, say Mass, or visit the sick and carry on his work as usual, such desires are pointless, since at the time they cannot be realized; they merely take the place of those he should have, namely, to be patient, resigned, mortified, obedient and submissive in his sufferings, which is God's will for him at the time. But often enough our desires are like those of a woman with child who wishes for cherries in the autumn and fresh grapes in the spring. I strongly disapprove of those who waste their time in desiring to lead a life unsuited to their present duty or incompatible with their state of life, for this only dissipates their hearts and makes them weak in doing what is necessary. If I, as a bishop, desire the solitude of a Carthusian I am wasting my time and this desire takes the place of the desire I should have to carry out my present work properly. I would not even wish anyone to desire greater talent or better judgement, for such desires are useless and take the place of the desire everyone should have to cultivate whatever talents he already possesses; instead of desiring new means of serving God, he should rather desire to make good use of those already at his disposal. All this refers to such *desires* as occupy the heart; as far as mere *wishes* are concerned, these are harmless, so long as we do not have too many. Desire crosses only in so far as you have borne well those that have been sent already, for it is self-deception to desire martyrdom when you have not even the fortitude to bear with some insult. The devil often encourages us to desire what is far away or impossible of fulfilment, to distract us from what is present and from occasions, no matter how trivial, which we could turn to good use. We imagine ourselves fighting the monsters of Africa and meanwhile allow ourselves to be overcome by the little serpents which really lie in our path. To desire temptations would be rash; instead we should prepare our hearts to meet them with courage and overcome them when they do come. Too great a variety of foods, especially if we eat too much, always overburdens the stomach, and injures it, if it is weak; in the same way, to fill the soul with spiritual desires would overburden it; to glut it with worldly desires would ruin it.

A soul once purified and free from evil inclinations has a great appetite for spiritual things, desiring, as one famished, countless practices of devotion, mortification, penance, humility, charity and prayer; such a good appetite, Philothea, is a good sign, but consider whether your digestion can cope with it all. You should rather choose with the help of your confessor such desires as can be put into practice here and now; when you have done that God will send you others which in their turn you can put into practice without wasting your time. This does not mean that you should relinquish any of your good desires, but merely that you should put them into practice in due order, locking them away in some corner of your heart while you give your attention to those which can be made to bear fruit in the present moment. This applies both to spiritual things and to worldly things. To act otherwise is to live in a constant state of restlessness and anxiety.

38. ADVICE TO THOSE WHO ARE MARRIED

MAN will leave his father and mother and will cling to his wife, and the two will become one flesh. Yes, those words are a high mystery, and I am applying them here to Christ and his Church.[1] *Marriage, in every way, must be held in honour.*[2] It must be held in honour by everyone, even, with humility, by virgins; in all persons, for it is equally holy in rich and poor; in every way, for its origin, its end, its advantages, and its matter and form, are all holy. It is the nursery of Christianity, peopling the earth with faithful souls who will complete the number of the elect in heaven; and the preservation of its sanctity is of the highest importance to society as being its very foundation, root and source. Would to God that his beloved Son were invited to every marriage as he was to that in Cana; then the wine of his consolations and blessings would never be wanting, as often happens at the beginning when Adonis and Venus are invited in the place of Christ and his mother.

Those who wish for a happy marriage should consider the dignity and holiness of this sacrament; if, instead, they concern themselves with rowdy entertainments, feasting and speeches, we should not be surprised if their marriages turn out badly. Above all I exhort those

[1] Eph. 5. 31, 32.   [2] Heb. 13. 4.

who are married to practise that mutual love so much recommended by the Holy Spirit in the Scriptures. Yet it is not enough to say: "Practise mutual love", for the turtle doves do as much; nor to say: "Have human love for each other", for pagans do that well enough; I would rather say in the words of St Paul: *You who are husbands must shew love to your wives, as Christ shews love to the Church;*[1] wives, love your husbands as the Church loves Christ." Eve was given to Adam as his wife *by God;* in the same way it is *God* who, with his invisible hand, has fashioned the sacred bond of your marriage and given you to each other; so that your mutual love should be altogether holy, sacred and divine.

The first effect of this love is the indissoluble union of your hearts. If two pieces of fir are joined together with strong glue, it is easier to break them than to separate them; but Christ unites husband and wife with his own blood in so strong a union that it should be more difficult to separate them than to separate the soul from the body; not as far as the physical union is concerned, but as far as the spiritual union of heart, affection and love is concerned.

The second effect of this love should be an inviolable mutual fidelity. In the marriage ceremony the Church, through the priest, blesses the wedding ring and by giving it first to the man symbolizes the seal it sets upon his heart by this sacrament, as, of old, seals were engraved upon the ring itself, closing his heart to the love or even the name of any other woman so long as his wife shall live; then the bridegroom places the ring on the finger of his bride in testimony that her heart, too,

[1] Eph. 5. 25.

is closed to love for any other man so long as he whom God has given her is still on earth.

The third fruit of marriage is the procreation and proper education of children. What an honour that God, wishing to multiply those who may bless and praise him for ever, should make husband and wife his co-operators in this work by the procreation of the bodies into which like drops from heaven he infuses the souls, creating them at that very moment.

Husbands, preserve a tender, constant and heartfelt love for your wives, for that was God's purpose in creating the first woman from that side of the first man nearest his heart. Your wives' weakness and frailty, whether bodily or spiritual, should move you rather to loving compassion than to any disdain, God having created them in such a way that their very dependence on you commands their honour and respect, and that though they are your companions, you may still be in authority over them. Wives, love the husbands given you by God tenderly and affectionately yet with reverence and respect, for God created them as the more vigorous and dominant sex willing that woman should depend upon man, bone of his bone and flesh of his flesh,[1] fashioned from a rib under his arm as a sign that she should be subject to his guiding hand; a subjection to which Holy Scripture binds you, yet renders easy, wishing your submission to be through love, and your husband's authority exercised through love, tenderness and gentleness. *You who are husbands*, says St Peter, *must use marriage considerately, paying homage to woman's sex as weaker than your own.*[2] While I exhort you to increase the mutual love you have for

[1] Cf. Gen. 2. 23.   [2] 1 Pet. 3. 7

each other, beware lest it develop into jealousy, for as worms breed in the ripest and most delicate fruits so jealousy breeds in the most ardent and affectionate love of husband and wife, gradually spoiling it and corrupting it by engendering disputes, arguments and even separation. But this can never happen when their mutual love is rooted in true virtue, such things being a clear indication that love is to some degree base and sensual, springing from a heart imperfect in virtue, inconstant and suspicious. To boast of jealousy is no proof of the goodness, purity and perfection of love but rather of its weakness and imperfection. Perfect love presupposes complete confidence in the virtue of the person we love, while jealousy presupposes a lack of confidence. A husband who wishes his wife to be faithful should set her a good example. "What right have you to expect your wife to be chaste", says St Gregory Nazianzen, "if you are not chaste yourself? How ask of her what you yourself are not prepared to give?" If you wish her to be pure you must be pure yourself. As St Paul says: *Each of you must learn to control his own body, as something holy and held in honour.*[1] But, on the other hand, if your example encourages her to be unfaithful, you should not be surprised at the disgrace this brings on you. Since a wife's honour and purity are inseparably bound up with her modesty and chastity, she should guard her good reputation jealously and never allow it to be tarnished by any kind of loose behaviour. Fear anything, no matter how small, which may affect it, and allow no one to trifle your affections. Suspect anyone who praises your beauty or your charm, for those who praise what is not for sale are usually strongly

[1] I Thess. 4.4.

tempted to steal it. If anyone, in addition to praising you, criticizes your husband, he adds insult to injury, clearly not only wishing to ruin you but considering you already half ruined, since a bargain is half concluded with a second merchant when the first merchant is unsatisfactory.

The age-old custom among women of wearing earrings of clustered pearls arises, according to Pliny, from the pleasure occasioned by the sound of their tinkling; but since God's servant Isaac sent earrings to the chaste Rebecca as first pledge of his love, I am of the opinion that such ornaments worn by a wife mystically signify that her ears are her husband's first possession, and that they are carefully guarded from all save the sweet and delightful music of pure and modest words which are the orient pearls mentioned in the Gospels; for we must always remember that, as I have said, poison enters the soul through the ears as it enters the body through the mouth.

Love wedded to fidelity gives birth to a confident intimacy, so that we find saintly husbands and wives making abundant use of mutual caresses as chaste as they are loving, as tender as they are sincere, as in the case of Isaac and Rebecca, the most pure couple in ages past. Abimelech, looking in at their window, saw them caressing one another in such a way that, though there was no immodesty, he realized that they were obviously husband and wife.

St Louis, as austere with himself as he was tenderly loving towards his wife, was blamed, almost, for being too lavish in this way, though he should rather have been praised for knowing how to bend his great and martial spirit to expressions of affection so necessary to the preservation of mutual love, for though they do not create this bond they are a delightful means of augmenting it.

St Monica dedicated her son, St Augustine, to the faith and to God's glory before he was born, so that, as he says himself, "he had already tasted the salt of God in his mother's womb",[1] an example which all Christian mothers should follow: offering the fruit of their womb to God even before they bring it forth. God, who accepts the offerings of a humble and willing heart, usually furthers a mother's aspirations at such a time as was the case with the mothers of Samuel, St Thomas Aquinas, St Andrew of Fiesole and many others.

St Bernard's mother, worthy of such a son, used to take her new-born children in her arms and offer them to our Lord, after which she cherished them as sacred and entrusted to her, now, by God, with such happy results that all seven of them became very holy.

As soon as children have grown to the use of reason their parents should inspire their hearts with the fear of the Lord, as did St Louis' mother, Queen Blanche, by often saying to him, "My dear child, I would much rather see you die before my very eyes than see you commit a single mortal sin". These words were so deeply impressed on his soul that, on his own testimony, he remembered them and strived to live up to them every day of his life.

We often refer to a race or a family as a "house"; the Jews called the raising of a family "the building of a house", for in this sense God is said to have *built houses*[2] for the midwives of Egypt. All this goes to show that to build a house does not mean to build a luxurious

---

[1] *Confessions*, I, ii.   [2] Exod. I. 21.

residence but to found a virtuous and God fearing family, sparing no sacrifice to do so, for children are their parents' *crown*.[1]

St Monica fought so fervently and consistently against the evil inclinations in her son St Augustine, following him over land and sea, that in the end he was more the child of her tears shed in converting his soul than of her blood in bearing his body.

St Paul assigns the *care of the house*[2] to the wife, so that many are of the opinion that her devotion is more profitable to the family than her husband's since she comes into closer contact with them than he can ever do, and so is in a better position to influence them by her virtuous example. For the same reason Solomon, in his Proverbs, makes the happiness of the household depend upon the care and industry of the vigorous wife he describes.[3]

In the book of Genesis we read that when Isaac found that his wife Rebecca was barren, *he prayed to the Lord for her* (or according to the Hebrew *besought the Lord opposite her*, since they prayed opposite one another in their oratory), *and his prayer was answered*.[4]

The union of husband and wife through devotion is the closest union of all and the most fruitful, and one to be mutually encouraged. Certain fruits, like quince, have so acid a juice that they are only palatable when preserved in sugar; others, like cherries and apricots, are so soft that they too will keep only if thy are preserved in sugar. Wives should be only too glad to see their husbands devout, for a man is severe, rough and harsh without the sugar of devotion; husbands should feel the same about their wives, for a woman without

[1] Prov. 17. 6. [2] Titus 2. 5. [3] Cf. Prov. 31. [4] Gen. 25. 21.

devotion is very frail and inconstant, so that her virtue is only too easily tarnished.

St Paul says that *the unbelieving husband is sanctified by the believing wife; and the unbelieving wife is sanctified by the believing husband,*[1] the close bond of marriage making it easy for the one to influence the other. How much better, then, when they mutually sanctify one another in the *fear of the Lord*.

Mutual support should be such that they never allow themselves to be angry both at the same time, so that all strife and dissension between them may be avoided. Bees flee a place loud with the clamour of voices and in the same way the Holy Spirit will not remain in a house which echoes with the sound of constant recriminations, disputes and wrangling. St Gregory Nazianzen tells us that, in his time, married couples used to make a feast-day of their wedding anniversary and I would like to see this custom revived so long as it is not made an occasion for worldly indulgence. Rather should it be celebrated by husband and wife going to confession and Communion together, invoking God's blessing on their married life, and renewing their good resolutions to sanctify it more and more by increasing their mutual love and fidelity; drawing new strength from God to fulfil the duties of their state.

39. THE SANCTITY OF THE MARRIAGE-BED

THE marriage-bed must be kept free from stain,[2] says St Paul; in other words, free from all impurity, as God ordained it in Eden, when it was free from the disorder of inordinate desire until the fall.

---

[1] I Cor. 7. 14.   [2] Heb. 13. 4.

There is a parity between the pleasures of marriage and those of eating, both being physical, though the former, because more sensual and intense, are referred to as carnal. What I cannot say of the one I will explain in terms of the other.

1. Eating is ordained to preserve and nourish life; to eat simply for this end is good, holy and obligatory; similarly what is necessary in marriage for the procreation of children, this being its primary end, is good and holy.

2. To eat, not to preserve life, but to promote that mutual friendship and concord we owe one another is in itself both just and lawful. Now St Paul refers to the mutual and lawful satisfaction of husband and wife as a *debt*[1] and a debt so binding that he will exempt neither party from paying it without the free and willing consent of the other, not even for the sake of devotion;[2] how much less then may either party withhold payment from anger, disdain or from some captious pretension to virtue!

3. When we eat with others to fulfil the duty of mutual intercourse we should do so freely, without constraint, and with some show of appetite; in the same way the marriage debt should always be paid freely and faithfully and as if hoping for children, even though, for some reason, this may not be possible.

4. To eat for neither of these reasons but merely for the pleasure of satisfying our appetite is permissible but not commendable, for mere pleasure is not a sufficient motive to make an action praiseworthy.

5. To eat, not merely to satisfy one's appetite, but immoderately and to excess, is more or less blameworthy, according to the excess.

[1] 1 Cor. 7. 3.   [2] Cf. Chapter on Holy Communion.

6. Such excess may either consist in eating too much or arise from how often and in what manner we eat.

Strange to say, Philothea, though honey is the bees' true nourishment, it may nevertheless be so harmful as to make them ill, as when they overeat in the spring; or it may lead to their death, as when they get their head and wings covered with it.

Marital intercourse is certainly holy, lawful and praiseworthy in itself and profitable to society, yet in certain circumstances it can prove dangerous, as when through excess the soul is made sick with venial sin, or through the violation and perversion of its primary end, killed by mortal sin; such perversion, detestable in proportion to its departure from the true order, being always mortal sin, for it is never lawful to exclude the primary end of marriage which is the procreation of children.

It may happen, for example, through sterility or pregnancy, that conception is not possible, in which case marital intercourse does not cease to be lawful and holy so long as the law governing the primary end of marriage is not violated, for in no circumstances is this permissible. We are informed in the book of Genesis that the shameful act committed by Onan in his marriage was *detestable* in God's sight,[1] and though certain heretics (far more blameworthy than the Cynics referred to by St Jerome in his commentary on *Ephesians*) have tried to prove that it was Onan's intention which displeased God, the Scriptures state otherwise, making it clear that what was detestable in God's sight was the very act itself.

7. It is the mark of a mean, vulgar and ignoble

[1] Gen. 38. 6—10.

196

spirit to dwell on the thought of food before meal times or worse to dwell on it afterwards, to discuss it and wallow in the remembered pleasures of every mouthful.

Those whose minds dwell before dinner on the spit, and after on the dishes, are fit only to be scullions; as St Paul says, *their own hungry bellies are the god they worship.*[1]

Those of noble mind think of food only when they sit down to table, and afterwards they wash their hands and rinse their mouth to rid themselves of the smell and the taste.

The elephant, not only the largest but the most intelligent of animals, provides us with an excellent example.

It is faithful and tenderly loving to the female of its choice, mating only every third year and then for no more than five days, and so secretly as never to be seen, until, on the sixth day, it appears and goes at once to wash its whole body in the river, unwilling to return to the herd until thus purified.

Such good and modest habits are an example to husband and wife in the sense that they should not allow themselves to become attached to the physical pleasures of marriage, but having enjoyed them they should, as it were, wash and purify their feelings and their heart as soon as possible, the more easily to give themselves to more lofty and spiritual things.

To do this is to fulfil St Paul's counsel to the Corinthians: *The time is drawing to an end; nothing remains, but for those who have wives to behave as though they had none;*[2] for according to St Gregory a married man behaves as though he had no wife in so far as he

---

[1] Phil. 3. 19.   [2] 1 Cor. 7. 29.

enjoys the pleasures of marriage without allowing them to divert him from more spiritual things; and the same applies to the wife.

St Paul also says: *Those who take advantage of what the world offers must not take full advantage of it.*[1] We should, then, use the things of the world as our state of life demands but in such a way that we are not attached to them, remaining as free and ready to serve God as if we made no use of them at all.

"Man's great misfortune", says St Augustine, "is that he seeks to enjoy what he should merely use, and to use what he should merely enjoy."

We may enjoy spiritual things but only use material ones, for to make them a matter for mere enjoyment is to debase our rational nature to the level of the beasts.

I think I have said all I wished to say, and made clear, without saying it, what I did not wish to say!

40. ADVICE TO WIDOWS

GIVE widows their due, if that name really belongs to them,[2] wrote St Paul to Timothy, his instruction applying to all bishops. To be *a true widow* these conditions must be fulfilled:

1. That she be a widow in spirit as well as in fact, absolutely resolved to preserve her widowhood inviolate. She is only a widow in the sense that she is cut off from the pleasures of marriage if she in bent on a second marriage, and is already married in desire.

If she is resolved on true widowhood the consecration of her body to God by a vow of chastity will enhance

[1] 1 Cor. 7. 31   [2] 1 Tim. 5. 3

her state and greatly strengthen her resolve, for, know-ing that she cannot break her vow without losing heaven, she will be so jealous of its fulfilment that she will not entertain for a moment the merest thought of marriage, so that her vow forms a strong defence against anything contrary to her resolution.

St Augustine advises Christian widows to make such a vow, while Origen goes even further, advising *wives* to vow themselves to a chaste widowhood in the event of their husbands' death so that even while they enjoy the pleasures of marriage they may anticipate the merit of such widowhood.

A vow brings with it an increase of courage for its fulfilment, makes what is done in consequence of it more pleasing to God, and not only consecrates the fruits of our good will to God, but the very will itself, the tree from which they spring.

By simple chastity we merely *lend* our body to God while retaining the freedom to enjoy the pleasures of marriage later on; by a vow of chastity we *give* our body to God irrevocably, absolutely; becoming his slave in a service which surpasses royalty.

As I strongly approve of the advice of the great men I have mentioned, I would like those who happily desire to follow it to do so firmly, with prudence and devotion, but only after counting the cost, invoking God's help and obtaining the advice of a wise and devout con-fessor, for then their efforts will bear more fruit.

2. She must renounce re-marriage purely and simply in order to centre all her affections on God and to give her heart to him entirely; for if she remains a widow for any other motive, for example that her wealth may go to her children, she may have *something to be proud of* but

certainly *not in God's sight*,[1] for such glory pertains only to what is done for his sake.

3. She must voluntarily renounce worldly pleasures, for St Paul says: *The widow who lives in luxury would be alive and dead both at once*;[2] for a widow to take pleasure, for example, in being courted, praised and flattered; to be attached to balls, dances and parties; to delight in fine dresses, perfumes and jewellery—all this is a sign that though she may be alive in body her soul is dead.

It matters little whether the sign outside the Inn of Adonis (worldly love) be a plume of white feathers, or a black crepe veil, . . . in fact the latter may be used to enhance the effect of the former; . . . a widow, because she knows from experience how to capture a man's heart, is able to set snares all the more alluring.

The widow that seeks such futile pleasures is *alive and death both at once*, possessing only the appearance of widowhood.

Pruning-time has come; we can hear the turtle-dove cooing already, there at home.[3] All who wish to be devout must prune away the superfluous things of the world, but this is particularly necessary in the case of a true widow who, like a faithful turtle dove, has but recently been mourning and weeping over the loss of her husband.

When Noemi returned from Moab to Bethlehem the women of the town who had known her as a bride said to one another: *Is not this Noemi*? But she replied: *Call me not Noemi, for that means comely and beautiful, but call me Mara, for the Lord has filled my soul with bitterness.*[4] She said this because her husband was dead. A

[1] Rom. 4. 2.   [2] 1 Tim. 5. 6.   [3] Cant. 2. 12.   [4] Cf. Ruth 1. 19,20

devout widow should, like Noemi, desire to be considered neither comely nor beautiful but be content to be as
God desires: humble and holy in his sight.

Lamps filled with aromatic oil are yet more fragrant
when their light has been extinguished, and the chastity
of a widow whose married love was pure is all the more
fragrant when the light which was her husband has been
extinguished by death. It is natural for a wife to love her
husband while he is alive, and to desire no other love
when he is gone; such love is the mark of a true widow.
It is no strange thing for a wife to trust in God while she
has her husband's support, but to do so when deprived
of that support is worthy of great praise, and manifests
more clearly the perfection of her virtue.

A widow with children dependent on her for help and
guidance, particularly with regard to their spiritual and
temporal needs, should not consider leaving them;
St Paul says quite clearly that she is bound to fulfil her
obligations: *the man who makes no provision for those
nearest him, above all his own family, has contradicted
the teaching of the faith, and indeed does worse than the
unbelievers do.*[1] But if they no longer need her care she
should direct all her thoughts and aspirations to her
own advancement in the love of God.

Unless it is absolutely necessary, as a matter of
conscience, she should take no part in lawsuits but
rather conduct her affairs in the most peaceful (even
though perhaps not the most profitable) way, for the
fruits of such anxious labour must be very great to
outweigh the fruits of tranquillity. Quite apart from
the fact that lawsuits and so on disturb the heart, they
often lay it open to the enemies of chastity, encouraging

[1] 1 Tim. 5. 8.

behaviour neither devout nor pleasing to God in order to court those whose help she needs in the furtherance of her cause.

A widow should devote herself to prayer, her words reserved principally for God, to whom her love belongs. As iron flies to the magnet once a counter attraction is removed so should her heart fly to God once her husband is dead; before, she could not give herself entirely to God, now she can follow the attraction of his divine love and hasten after him, allured by the very fragrance of his perfumes, saying: "Now, O Lord, that I am all my own, I give myself to be all thine" and, with the Spouse of the Canticles: *Draw me after thee where thou wilt.*[1]

A true widow should posses the virtue of modesty; should renounce honours, rank, position, titles and similar vanities; should comfort the afflicted and instruct young women in devotion, striving to be, herself, a perfect example. Her dress should be adorned with neatness and simplicity; her actions with humility and love; her words with sincerity and gentleness; her eyes with modesty; her heart centred only on Christ Crucified.

Like a March violet, the true widow spreads about her an incomparable sweetness by the fragrance of her devotion, while remaining hidden for the most part beneath the broad leaves of her humility; the sombre hues of her dress witness her austerity; she flowers in cool uncultivated spots, flying the claims of worldly society, to guard the freshness of her heart from the desire for riches, honours and even wordly love, with which it might otherwise be inflamed. *Blessed is she*, says St Paul, *if she remains as she is.*[2]

[1] Cant. I. 3.   [2] I Cor. 7. 40.

I could say more but it can all be summed up by advising a widow, jealous for the honour of her state, to read carefully the beautiful letters of St Jerome to Furia and Salvia and to those other women happy enough to be his spiritual daughters.

There is no more to add except this one last piece of advice: a true widow should never blame or criticize those who marry a second or even a third or fourth time, for in some cases God ordains this for his greater glory. Rather should she ever bear in mind what has been taught of old, that in heaven the rank both of virgins and of widows will depend on their humility.

41. ADVICE TO VIRGINS

IF you aspire to a temporal marriage keep your first love jealously for your first husband, for I consider it deceitful to give him a heart that is soiled, dissipated and worn out with too much love instead of a heart that is whole and entire.

If, on the other hand, you aspire to the pure virginal nuptials of a spiritual marriage you should desire perpetual virginity and keep your love as inviolate as possible for your Divine Spouse, to whom we owe the first fruits of everything, but most of all the first fruits of our love. Being purity itself he loves purity above all else.

For the rest you should read the epistles of St Jerome which contain all you need, and, since obedience is a condition of your life, choose a guide under whose direction you may dedicate yourself more devoutly, body and soul, to God.

PART FOUR

OVERCOMING TEMPTATIONS

I. WORLDLY WISDOM

As soon as worldly people see you bent upon the devout life they will shower you with mockery and detraction. The more malicious will attribute your change to hypocrisy and insincerity, saying you have turned to God only because the world has disappointed you. Your friends will raise countless objections which they consider wise and charitable, saying that it will only make you morose and unbearable; that it will discredit you in the eyes of the world; that you will grow old before your time; that your domestic affairs will suffer; that those who live in the world must live accordingly and that you can get to heaven without all these mysteries and so on. All this is but stupid and empty babbling, Philothea. They are interested neither in your health nor your affairs. *"If you belonged to the world"*, says our Lord, *"the world would know you for its own and love you; it is because you do not belong to the world that the world hates you.*[1] We have seen men and women spend, not only the whole night, but several nights in succession, playing cards or chess. Is there anything more dull, miserable and absurd than this? And yet it does not disturb worldly people in the least; but if we spend an hour in meditation or are noticed

[1] John 15. 19.

getting up in the morning earlier than usual to go to Holy Communion, they send for a doctor at once to cure us of melancholy and jaundice! They can spend thirty nights in dancing without experiencing any ill effects but if they have to spend one Christmas night in watching they are full of coughs and complaints the next day. It is quite obvious that the world is an unjust judge; gracious and forbearing with its own children, but harsh and rigorous with the children of God.

Only the worldly stand well with the world; we can never satisfy its caprices. *When John came, he would neither eat nor drink, and they said of him that he was possessed. When the Son of Man came, he ate and drank with them, and of him they said: Here is a glutton; he loves wine.*[1]

The worldly will be scandalized, Philothea, if we condescend to laugh, play or dance in their company, but if we refuse, they will call us melancholy hypocrites. If we dress well they will attribute it to a bad motive; if we dress simply they will attribute it to meanness. They will call our joy dissipation, our self-denial sadness, their jaundiced gaze never satisfied. They will magnify our imperfections into sins, count our venial sins as mortal and our sins of frailty as sins of malice.

Charity is kind,[1] they are spiteful; charity never thinks evil, they always do; and if they cannot find fault with our actions, they censure our intentions. It does not matter to the wolf whether the sheep are black or white, whether they have horns or not, he will devour them if he can. The worldly are against us whatever we do; if we are in the confessional for a long time, they will express surprise that we have so much to confess; if

---

[1] Matt. 11. 18, 19.   [1] 1 Cor. 13. 4, 5.

we are only in there for a short time they will say that we have not confessed everything. They will watch us carefully; one word of anger and they will say we have an ungovernable temper; if we show prudence in our affairs they will say we are avaricious; if we are gentle they will call us foolish, while as for them, their anger is courage, their avarice economy, their over-familiarity honest fun; spiders always spoil the honeycomb. We must ignore such blindness, Philothea; let them cry out like owls trying to disturb the birds of day as much as they like while we go serenely on our way, unwavering in our resolves; our very perseverance will convince them that we have dedicated ourselves to God and embraced a devout life. Comets are almost as bright as planets, but being only transitory they soon disappear, whereas planets shine constantly. In the same way, hypocrisy is hard to distinguish from true virtue externally; the test lies in the fact that hypocrisy is inconstant and vanishes like smoke whereas true virtue is ever firm and constant. To meet with reproaches and criticisms at the beginning of our spiritual life helps to establish our devotion, for it prevents us from falling into pride and vanity which kill our works as soon as they come to birth, as the midwives of Egypt killed the male Israelites under Pharaoh. *We are crucified to the world*[1] and the world should stand crucified to us; it counts us fools; let us count it demented.

2. COURAGE IN DEVOTION

THOUGH light is beautiful and lovely it dazzles our eyes if we have been in darkness for any length of time; we

[1] Cf. Gal. 6. 14.

are always ill at ease in a strange country no matter how gracious and courteous its inhabitants, until we become familiar with them. It may well happen, Philothea, that having embarked on this new life, your soul may feel ill at ease and that you experience a sense of sadness and discouragement in bidding farewell to the follies and vanities of the world; be patient a little while, it is of no importance, only the discomfort of unfamiliarity; as soon as it has worn off you will experience abundant consolation.

At first you may regret losing the empty glory with which flattering fools rewarded your vanity, but would you exchange it for the eternal glory with which God will in truth reward you? The futile amusements of the past may return to tempt your heart back to them; are you courageous enough to buy them back at the price of eternal happiness? Persevere and certainly your heart will soon be filled with such pleasant and delightful consolations that you will count the pleasures in the world but gall in comparison with their sweetness, and a single day of devotion preferable to a thousand years of worldliness.

Seeing the mountain of Christian perfection towering above you, you may doubt your ability to climb it; but take courage, Philothea. Unformed bees are called nymphs and at this stage are unable to fly for honey to the flowers or hills or mountains, but little by little, feeding on the honey prepared for them, they grow wings and soon are sufficiently strong to fly in search of fresh honey far and wide. True, we are no more than such nymphs in devotion, we cannot fly as we would like to the mountain tops of Christian perfection; nevertheless we are beginning to take shape by feeding on our desires and resolutions; we are beginning to grow wings and so may be confident that one day we shall be able to fly. Meanwhile, we must feed on the abundant honey provided by former spiritual writers, and ask God to give us *wings like a dove*,[1] that we may be able to fly in this life and reach eternal rest hereafter.

3. TEMPTATION AND CONSENT

IMAGINE a young princess, Philothea, whose husband loves her dearly; then imagine that some evil man, desiring to commit adultery with her, sends a messenger to make known his love and to further his desire.

First of all the messenger reveals to the princess his master's proposal.

Secondly, she either takes pleasure in it or not.

Thirdly, she either consents or not.

In the same way, the world, the flesh and the devil send tempting suggestions to a soul espoused to Christ. First the sin is proposed; secondly the soul is either pleased or displeased; thirdly the soul either consents or refuses. These three steps to sin—temptation, pleasure in the temptation, consent—are not always easy to distinguish but they are clear enough in the case of grave sin.

Temptation of any sort, no matter how long it endures, cannot make us displeasing to God so long as we take no pleasure in it and do not yield; to be tempted is something passive, not active, and no blame attaches to us while we are opposed to it. St Paul suffered temptations of the flesh for years without being displeasing to God,

[1] Ps. 54. 7.

on the contrary, they were a means of promoting God's glory. Blessed Angela of Foligno's account of similar temptations moves us to compassion; St Francis and St Benedict suffered such great temptations that one cast himself naked upon thorns and the other into the snow to overcome them, gaining instead of losing grace.

Have great courage, Philothea, in the midst of temptations, knowing that your displeasure is the sign of your victory, for it is one thing to experience temptations and another to consent to them; we may still *feel* them even though they displease us, but we can *consent* to them only if they please us, this pleasure being the first step to consent.

Let the enemies of the soul lay their alluring snares before us as often as they like; let them knock for admittance at the door of our heart as long as they like; let them make as many proposals as they like; so long as we are resolved to take no pleasure in such things, we can no more offend God than the princess could offend her husband by receiving a message in which she took no pleasure. There is this difference however: the princess can dismiss the messenger once for all, we cannot dismiss the temptation in the same way but we can always refuse consent; so no matter how long the temptation lasts it can do us no harm unless we take pleasure in it.

Even with regard to this pleasure, we must remember that there is a superior and an inferior part of the soul; the inferior part does not always follow the superior part, but often goes its own way, taking pleasure in the temptation without and against the consent of the superior part, a conflict to which St Paul refers, when he says *the impulses of nature and the impulses of the spirit are at war with one another;*[1] and that *the disposition of the lower self raises war against the disposition of the conscience,*[2] and so on. Have you ever noticed a large brazier, Philothea, in which the fire is overlaid with ashes? Go back hours later and it will be hard to discover a few glowing embers; nevertheless they are there, and they will serve to kindle the whole fire again. It is the same with charity, the essence of our spiritual life; when the inferior part of the soul is overlaid with terrible temptations, the whole soul seems covered with ashes, the love of God reduced to a spark in the very centre of the heart and in the very depths of the soul, so imperceptible that it hardly seems to be there at all; yet it is there; that resolution never to consent in the midst of temptations which flood the soul and body; that displeasure, in spite of an outward sense of pleasure, which proves that though temptations may be all about the will they have not been admitted and that the pleasure, because involuntary, can be no sin.

4. TWO EXAMPLES

As this matter is of such importance I make no excuse for explaining it further.

St Jerome mentions the case of a young man tied down upon a luxurious bed with silken bonds while a sensuous woman, detailed by a tyrant to shake his constancy, made love to him, provoking him with every means at her command.

Do you imagine that his body did not respond to her touch? That his senses and his imagination were not possessed by what he experienced? There can be no

[1] Gal. 5. 17.   [2] Cf. Rom. 7. 23.

doubt of that, yet in spite of it all, in the midst of such a storm of temptations, such a flood of sensual pleasure, he proved the victory of his heart and his will's refusal to consent. Experiencing the complete revolt of all except his tongue, he bit it off and spat it in the face of this woman who was tormenting his soul more cruelly with pleasure than the torturers had with pain, as had been the tyrant's intention, torture being despaired of as a means of overcoming him.

There is an admirable account of a similar struggle in the case of St Catherine of Siena, when God allowed the devil to try her purity with every means in his power short of touching her.

First he assailed her heart with impure suggestions and then, to provoke her further, he appeared with other evil spirits in the form of men and women, and committed countless acts of sensual pleasure in her sight, inviting her to take part.

Although all this was exterior to her, it stirred her senses and made such a deep impression on her heart that, as she herself confessed, only her superior will could resist the storm of impure pleasure which filled it.

These temptations endured for a long time until one day our Lord appeared to her.

"Where were you, my Saviour", she asked, "when my heart was flooded with such darkness and impurity?"

"Within your heart, my daughter", he replied.

"How is that possible when it was so filled with obscenity?" she asked. "How could you dwell in so unclean a place?"

"Tell me", said our Lord, "did such impure thoughts cause you pleasure or sadness; bitterness or delight?"

"The greatest sadness and bitterness", she replied.

"Who but I caused that sadness and bitterness in your heart?" he said; "I, who remained hidden in the depths of your soul? Be assured, my daughter, that had I not been present, those thoughts which assaulted your will so unsuccessfully would have prevailed, entered and been freely welcomed, bringing death to your soul. But being present I caused this displeasure and resistance in your heart and enabled you to reject the temptation with all your strength; and because this was not as much as you desired, you conceived an even greater detestation of the temptation, so that your struggles were a source of great spiritual profit, increasing your merit, your virtue and your strength."

Notice, Philothea, how the fire was covered with ashes, how temptation and pleasure entered the heart and encompassed the will; notice how the will alone, aided by our Saviour, by its very aversion, bitterness and hatred resisted the suggestions of evil and steadfastly refused to consent to the sins which besieged it on every side.

How distressing to one who loves God not to know whether he is present in the soul or not, to be uncertain if that love by which and for which we fight is still alive; but to be asked to suffer thus is the fairest flower of perfect heavenly love.

5. ENCOURAGEMENT IN TEMPTATION

GOD allows such great trials and temptations, Philothea, to befall only those whom he wishes to advance to a more powerful and excellent participation in his love. This result, however, does not necessarily follow, for it sometimes happens that having overcome these great temptations they afterwards give in to much smaller ones through lack of correspondence with divine grace. I say this so that, should you ever experience great temptation, you may recognize it as an extraordinary favour from God, manifesting his desire to exalt you in his sight.

Nevertheless you must always remain humble and diffident, not being too confident of your ability to overcome small temptations because you have overcome greater ones, for this ability depends entirely on constant fidelity to God. Whatever temptations you may experience and whatever pleasure they may occasion, as long as your will rejects both the temptation and the pleasure you need not be upset for you will not have offended God. If a man falls unconscious and gives no sign of life we place our hand on his heart; if we feel the least movement we judge him to be still alive and capable of being restored to consciousness by use of medicine or some other means. In the same way it sometimes happens that our soul seems to have lost use of its powers and to be bereft of spiritual life owing to the violence of temptation. If this is the case we must lay our hand upon our heart; in other words, consider if our will is still active in rejecting the temptation and pleasure as it should. As long as this is the case we may be assured that we still possess charity, which is the life of the soul, and that Jesus Christ our Saviour is present in our soul, though hidden and concealed; so that by means of continual prayer, the sacraments, and confidence in God, we shall regain the strength to live a good and happy life.

6. SINFUL TEMPTATION AND SINFUL PLEASURE

THE princess we have mentioned was not responsible for the dishonourable proposal made to her since we have presupposed that it was made against her will, but if, on the contrary, she had in any way encouraged the man who courted her, wishing to make love to him, she would obviously be responsible for the very proposal; and even if she then drew back she would still be worthy of blame and punishment.

A temptation may therefore be sinful because we are the cause of it; if, for example, I know that I easily lose my temper and swear when I gamble, and that such games are an occasion of sin, I sin as often as I take part in them, and am responsible for all the temptations I experience. In the same way, if I know that certain company is an occasion of temptation and sin and yet still choose to enter that company I am certainly responsible for all the temptations which follow. If the pleasure arising from the temptation can be avoided, to receive it is always a sin, the gravity of which depends on the degree and duration of its pleasure and consent. If the princess not only listens to the dishonourable proposal, but also, having done so, takes pleasure in thinking about it, she is certainly worthy of blame; for though she may not intend what is suggested, she has consented in her heart by the very fact that she has taken pleasure in the thought. To devote the heart of the body to what is wrong is always sinful, in fact, the sinfulness depends so essentially on the heart that there can be no bodily sin without it. When you are temped to some sin, consider if you voluntarily gave occasion to it, for in that case you sinned by exposing yourself to the risk; that is, if you could easily have avoided the occasion and if you foresaw or should have foreseen the temptation; but if this was not the case you are in no way guilty. As I have said, when the pleasure which follows a temptation could have been avoided, it is always to some extent sinful depending on how long it endures and on its cause.

A woman who takes pleasure in a flirtation which she has not encouraged is blameworthy if the pleasure arises from the flirtation itself; but if the person who flirts with her plays the lute beautifully and she takes pleasure, not in the flirtation, but in the sweet harmonies of the lute, there is no sin; though she should not dwell on this pleasure for long lest it extend to the flirtation itself. In the same way, if anyone suggests an ingenious and cunning way to revenge myself on an enemy and I simply take pleasure in the ingenuity of the plan and not in the thought of revenge, I do not sin at all; though, here again, I should not dwell too long on this pleasure lest it lead me to take pleasure in the thought of the revenge itself.

Sometimes a temptation takes us by surprise and we feel pleasure before we have had time to resist it; at the most this is a very light venial sin and only becomes more serious if, aware of the evil, we entertain the pleasure while we make up our mind whether to accept or reject it. It becomes more serious still if once aware of it we dwell on it for any length of time through downright negligence, without making any effort to reject it; but if we willingly and deliberately resolve to accept such pleasure, it is a grave sin if the temptation itself was grave. Hence it is gravely wrong for a woman to take pleasure in the thought of sinful love even though she may have no intention of yielding to her desires.

7. REMEDIES FOR GREAT TEMPTATIONS

As soon as you find yourself tempted, follow the example of children who when they see a wolf or a bear at large run at once to their parents' arms or at least call out to them for help and assistance; in other words, fly to the arms of God and implore his mercy and his aid, for this is the remedy recommended by our Lord when he says: *Pray, that you may not enter into temptation.*[1] If you find that the temptation still continues, or even grows stronger, hasten in spirit to embrace the Cross as if you saw Christ Crucified before your eyes; protest that you will never yield, ask him to help you, beg him to strengthen your resistance, and continue to do so as long as the temptation lasts. While doing so, never look at the temptation itself but only at our Lord; otherwise if the temptation is a strong one, it may cause you discouragement. Divert your mind from it by every good and lawful means you can; let them so occupy your heart as to drive out the evil suggestions arising from the temptation. The best remedy against temptations, whether they are great or small, is to open our hearts to our confessor, making all these suggestions, temptations and feelings known to him, for silence is the first condition the devil makes with a soul he wishes to seduce, in the same way that those who wish to seduce a woman or a young girl forbid her, from the first, to make their proposals known to husband or father. God, on the contrary, requires above all that we

[1] Matt. 26. 41.

should make them known to our superiors and our confessors. If, having done all this, the temptation still obstinately persists in troubling us and making us anxious there is nothing to do but remain obstinate ourselves in our refusal to consent, for as a girl cannot be married so long as she says "no", so the soul, no matter how harassed, can never be harmed so long as it refuses consent.

Never argue with the enemy; give him no answer save that of our Lord: *Away with thee, Satan; it is written, Thou shalt worship the Lord thy God, and serve none but him.*[1] A pure wife should answer not a word to one who makes an impure proposal to her, nor even look him in the face, but leave him at once, turning her heart towards her husband and renewing her promise of fidelity to him. In the same way, a devout soul when assailed by some temptation should waste no time in replying or arguing but simply turn at once towards Jesus Christ her Spouse, renewing her protestation of fidelity and her desire to be entirely his for ever.

8. RESISTING SMALL TEMPTATIONS

WE must fight great temptations with invincible courage, and our victory brings great profit, yet, to fight well against small temptations may be more profitable still. Though great temptations may surpass them in quality, small temptations are far more numerous and so the victory over them is comparable.

Wolves and bears are obviously more dangerous than flies yet they are less irritating and do not try our patience to the same extent; it is easy to refrain from

[1] Matt. 4. 10.

murder but hard to refrain from the anger which we are constantly tempted to express; easy to refrain from adultery yet hard to refrain from loving glances, expressions of mutual love, from soliciting favours and from flattery. It is easy to keep one's body for one's husband or wife but hard to keep one's heart; easy not to violate one's married love but hard to avoid what may injure it; easy to avoid stealing but hard to avoid envy; easy to avoid perjury but hard to avoid lying; easy never to get drunk yet hard always to be temperate; easy not to wish the death of another but hard never to wish him harm; easy never to defame him but hard never to despise him.

Temptations to anger, suspicion and jealousy, to envy, flirtation and frivolity; to vanity, insincerity and affectation; to deceit and impure thoughts, these are the very things which the devout must fight most resolutely. Prepare yourself for this battle, Philothea, with great care, assured that every small victory will merit another jewel in the crown of glory which God prepares for you in heaven. Fight valiantly against great temptations when they come your way but in the meantime defend yourself diligently against these smaller ones.

9. REMEDIES FOR SMALL TEMPTATIONS

TREAT such small temptations like flies and gnats which flutter about us and sometimes settle on the face; as we cannot be entirely rid of them our best defence is to remain undisturbed; they can annoy us but never harm us so long as we are firmly resolved to serve God. Despise such temptations without listening to them; treat them like flies; let them hover all around you and buzz about your ears as much as they like; when they settle on your heart and try to sting you, do not attack them or argue with them but merely drive them away quietly by making acts of love of God or of any other virtue; or if you have had time to recognize the real nature of the temptation, by an act of the contrary virtue; then turn your heart to Christ Crucified and in spirit kiss his feet by an act of love, for to persist in acts of the contrary virtue would be to dispute with the temptation.

An act of the love of God is the surest weapon against temptations great and small; for the love of God contains to an eminent degree the perfection of all the virtues and is the most perfect remedy for vice. Learn to seek peace in this remedy whenever temptations trouble you, and you will have no need to examine or consider them; moreover, the devil will be so terrified when he sees that these temptations lead you to make acts of the love of God that he will cease to trouble you. So much for these countless small temptations; to give more attention to them would only be a waste of time.

10. HOW TO STRENGTHEN YOUR HEART

FROM time to time consider what are your greatest weaknesses then adopt a way of life completely contrary in thought, word and deed. For example: if you find that you are inclined to be vain, consider the worthlessness of worldly things, the effect they will have on your conscience when you come to die, how unworthy they are of a generous heart, being no more than the playthings of a child, and so on. Deprecate vanity whenever you can, no matter what you feel, then honour will bind you to its opposite. We come to hate what we disparage though we were at first attached to it. Do humble, lowly tasks as often as possible, even though with apparent reluctance, for this will so weaken your vanity that when temptations come you will have less inclination to consent and more courage to resist.

If you find that you are inclined to be avaricious, consider the folly of this vice which makes us slaves of what was made to serve us; consider that you will have to leave all your possessions to someone else when you die; that he may squander them or use them to his ruin, and so on. Deprecate this vice, praise contempt of the world, go out of your way to give alms and perform acts of charity and let occasional opportunities of gain slip by.

If you are inclined to flirtation often consider how dangerous this is, both to yourself and to others; how unworthy to profane the soul's most noble affection for the sake of mere amusement; and that it is the mark of a frivolous spirit. Often praise purity and simplicity of heart, conforming your actions to your words as far as possible by avoiding affection and everything that even savours of flirtation. Finally, in time of peace, in other words when you are free from temptations, make acts of the contrary virtue, seeking out occasions if they do not present themselves, and in this way you will strengthen your heart for the future.

II. ANXIETY

ANXIETY is not only a temptation in itself, but a source of many others. Sadness is that sorrow we experience in face of some evil either exterior such as poverty, illness, contempt, or interior such as ignorance, dryness in prayer, repugnance or temptation. Such sadness makes us desire to escape evil and to have the means of escape, and rightly so, for we naturally desire what is good and avoid what we consider to be evil.

If we seek to be delivered for the love of God we will do so patiently, gently, humbly and peacefully, looking for our deliverance more from the goodness and providence of God than from our own efforts and labour. If we seek deliverance out of self-love it will be with eagerness and anxiety, as if it depended more upon ourselves than upon God. I do not say that we necessarily think so but that we act eagerly as if we did; and if we do not succeed at once, we become restless and impatient; but instead of overcoming the evil this only makes it worse. We become overwhelmed with anguish and distress, and feel so weak and discouraged that the evil seems incurable. You see then, Philothea, how that sadness, which is at first justified, leads to anxiety while anxiety in its turn increases sadness and makes it extremely dangerous.

This anxiety is the greatest evil that can befall us except sin, for just as revolt and sedition in a country cause havoc and sap its resistance to a foreign invasion, so we, when troubled and worried, are unable to preserve the virtues we have already acquired or resist the temptations of the devil who then diligently fishes, as they say, in troubled waters. Anxiety arises from a desire to be delivered from the evil we experience or to obtain some good for which we hope, yet nothing so aggravates the evil or impedes the good as this over-eagerness and anxiety. Birds remain ensnared because they flutter in their wild attempts to escape from the net, and in doing so get all the more entangled, so, when you desire to be delivered from some evil or to obtain some good, first strive, above all, for peace and tranquillity. First compose your judgement and your will and then seek to attain your end quietly and gently, taking the most suitable one at a time. *Gently* does not mean *negligently* but *without eagerness, anxiety and disquiet*, otherwise, instead of attaining your end, you will only make everything far worse and get more and more entangled.

I carry my life in my hands, yet am I ever mindful of thy law,[1] said David. Examine several times a day, but at least morning and evening, whether your soul really is in your hands or whether some passion or anxiety has taken possession of it; whether your heart is under control or has escaped and becomed carried away by inordinate love, hatred, envy, avarice, fear, weariness or joy; in which case you must, above all, recapture it and restore it to the presence of God, subjecting its feelings and desires to his will. We hold what is precious tightly in our hands for fear of losing it; so we should always say with this great king, "I fear to lose my soul, O God, therefore I carry it always in my hands, and so have not forgotten thy holy law".

Never allow desires, however trivial, to disquiet you, for that would only leave you with less resistance to the clamour of greater ones. When you experience disquiet, turn to God and resolve not to do what you desire until the disquiet has passed, unless it is something which cannot be deferred, in which case you must restrain, control and moderate your desire as far as possible with gentleness and tranquillity, acting according to reason,

[1] Ps. 118. 109.

not mere inclination. If you can make known your disquietude to your confessor, or at least to some good and faithful friend, be assured that you will at once find relief, for to reveal the sufferings of our heart has the same effect on the soul as blood-letting in the case of someone suffering from chronic fever . . . it is the best of all remedies. As St Louis advised his son: "If any trouble afflicts your heart, make it known at once to some good friend, and the strength you will gain from this will enable you to bear your trouble easily."

12. SADNESS

SUPERNATURAL *remorse*, says St Paul, *leads to an abiding and salutary change of heart, whereas the world's remorse leads to death.*[1] Sadness, then, may be good or evil, depending on its effect, though it produces many more evil effects than good, of which there are only two, compassion and repentance; whereas it produces six bad effects: anxiety, discouragement, anger, jealousy, envy, and impatience, which is why the wise man says: *Sadness has been the death of many, and no good ever came of it.*[2]

The devil takes advantage of sadness to tempt the good, striving to make them sorrowful in their virtue as he strives to make the wicked rejoice in their sins, and as he can only tempt us to evil by making it appear attractive, so he can only tempt us away from what is good by making it appear unattractive. He delights to see us sad and despondent because he is such himself for all eternity and wishes everyone to be as he is.

[1] 2 Cor. 7. 10.   [2] Ecclus. 30. 25.

Evil sadness disturbs the soul, leads to disquiet and inordinate fear, breeds distaste for prayer, clouds the mind, undermines our judgement, resolution and courage, and saps our energy. It is like a hard winter which robs the earth of its beauty and freezes every living thing, for it robs our soul of consolation and leaves it powerless and almost paralysed. If such sadness should come upon you, Philothea, make use of the following remedies: *Is one of you unhappy?* says St James, *let him fall to prayer*,[1] for prayer is the sovereign remedy, lifting the soul to God the source of all joy and consolation; make use of aspirations, either vocal or interior, which tend to confidence and love, for example: "O God so merciful and good!" "My loving Saviour!" "God of my heart, my joy and hope!" "My true spouse, the well-beloved of my soul", and so on.

Resist any tendency to sadness most vigorously and do not falter because your efforts seem to be made half-heartedly and without fervour, for the devil will cease to trouble you when he sees that instead of being wearied by sadness you continue your good works and gain all the more merits as a result. Sing spiritual canticles, for this practice has often forced the devil to abandon his efforts. Remember how David, by singing psalms, drove away the evil spirit which so oppressed Saul.

It is also very useful to keep yourself occupied with exterior works as varied as possible, to divert your mind from the cause of your sadness, to purify your heart and increase your fervour; for sadness makes us lukewarm. Express your devotion outwardly even though without sensible fervour; for example, embrace the crucifix, clasp it to your breast; kiss our Lord's hands and feet;

[1] James 5. 13.

raise your hands to heaven in supplication; make such acts of love and confidence as these: *All mine, my true love, and I all his.*[1] *Close my love is to my heart as the cluster of myrrh that lodges in my bosom all the night through.*[2] *Keeping watch for the fulfilment of thy promise, my eyes languish for comfort still delayed.*[3] O Jesus, be my Saviour and my soul shall live. *Who will separate me from thy love?*[4] and so on. A moderate use of the discipline is a good remedy for sadness, because voluntary physical suffering merits spiritual consolation, while the soul is diverted from its interior sufferings by these exterior ones. Holy Communion is an excellent remedy, for this bread will keep your strength from failing and rejoice your heart.[5] Your sadness, and all the feelings and temptations that spring from it, should be made known humbly and sincerely to your confessor; at such times spend as much time as possible in the company of spiritual persons. Finally, resign yourself into God's hands and strive to bear patiently the sadness which troubles you as a just punishment for the empty joys of the past; confident that, having tested you, God will deliver you from this trial.

13. SPIRITUAL AND SENSIBLE CONSOLATION

GOD maintains the world in existence in a state of continual change: day passes into night, spring into summer, summer into autumn, autumn into winter, and winter into spring, and no two days are ever exactly alike, some being cloudy, some rainy, some dry, some windy, a variety which makes the world all the more

[1] Cant. 2. 16.   [2] Cant. 1. 12.   [3] Ps. 181. 82.
[4] Cf. Rom. 8. 35.   [5] Cf. Ps. 103. 15.

beautiful. The same law of change applies to man, who has been called "an epitome of the world", for his state is ever changing, constantly in movement; his life on earth like waters which ebb and flow, sometimes lifted up by hope, sometimes depressed by fear, swept one way by consolation, another by affliction; no day, no hour, exactly the same.

It is well to remember this, for we must strive to preserve our equanimity in the midst of these various changes; though all should change about us we must remain immovable, our eyes and our hearts ever fixed on God. Whatever course a ship may take, north or south, east or west, no matter what wind sweeps it on, its compass will ever point towards the pole star. Even if our world, without or within, turns upside down, in sadness or in joy, in consolation or in bitterness, in peace or in affliction, darkness or light, temptation or tranquillity, whether we experience pleasure or weariness, dried up by the sun or refreshed by the dew, our compass, in other words our superior will, must always be fixed on God, our Creator and redeemer, our one and only good, towards whom our love forever carries us. *While we live*, says St Paul, *we live as the Lord's servants; when we die, we die as the Lord's servants.*[1] *Who will separate us from the love of Christ? Neither death nor life, neither what is present nor what is to come*, neither the height of consolation nor the depth of affliction, neither tenderness in devotion nor dryness in prayer, ought ever *to separate us from the love of God which comes to us in Christ Jesus our Lord.*[2] An inviolable resolution to tend always to God and his love will serve to preserve our equanimity in the midst of all the chang-

[1] Rom. 14. 8.   [2] Cf. Rom. 8. 35, 38, 39.

ing circumstances of our lives. It is said that bees preserve their balance in the air when caught in a storm by holding fast to little stones and so prevent themselves from being carried away, so we, by holding fast to the love of God, will preserve our balance in the midst of the storm of change, whether temporal or spiritual, whether within us or about us.

In addition to these general principles we need some particular advice.

1. Devotion does not consist in any feelings of pleasure, sadness, consolation or compassion which move us to tears and sighs and make our spiritual exercises pleasing and agreeable; for, Philothea, such feelings may be experienced by those who are still attached to sin and who consequently have no true love for God, much less any true devotion. Saul, intending to kill David, followed him into the desert of Engaddi; there he happened to enter, all alone, the very cave in which David and his men were concealed. David could quite easily have killed him but he spared his life, in fact he let Saul go without even revealing his presence, to avoid causing him fear, only calling out to him afterwards so that he might prove his innocence and let him know that he had him at his mercy. Remember how Saul showed that his heart was softened towards David; he wept aloud, called him his son, praised him, admitted his goodness, called down God's blessing on him, foretold his future greatness and begged mercy for his own descendants. He could not have shown more gentleness and tenderness of heart, and yet, in spite of it all, his heart had not really been changed and he continued to persecute David as cruelly as ever.

So some, when they consider the goodness of God and

the passion of our Lord, feel great tenderness of heart which causes them to weep and sigh, to pray and give thanks with such deep feeling that they appear to be very devout; but when put to the test such tears are found to be like summer showers, which fall abundantly upon the parched earth yet do not soak in and produce only toadstools; these tears and feelings of tenderness fall upon their vicious hearts without penetrating, and so are quite useless. I say useless because in spite of all this apparent devotion they would not restore a penny of their ill-gotten goods, renounce any of their evil inclinations or put themselves to the least inconvenience in the service of the Saviour for whom they have shed these tears; their feelings of devotion are no more in fact than toadstools; not only are they false devotion, they are often snares of the devil, who encourages them to make much of these consolations and take such satisfaction in them that they no longer seek true devotion, which is to do constantly, resolutely, promptly, and energetically whatever we know to be pleasing to God.

A child will weep to see his mother bled with a lancet but should she then ask him for an apple or some sugar plums that he has in his hand, he will not part with them. We usually act in the same way with regard to our feelings of devotion. We weep to see the lance thrust into our Lord's heart and it is right that we should do so; why, then, do we refuse to give him the apple we hold in our hands and which he asks for so earnestly, in other words, our heart, the only apple of love which he desires? Who do we not renounce, for his sake, those feelings of pleasure and consolation which he desires to pluck from our hands and cannot because they are our sugar plums and we prefer them to his heavenly grace? Such feeble, unstable and fruitless sentiments befit only little children! Devotion, then, does not consist in such feelings, which are often merely the result of our natural temperament, soft and impressionable, though sometimes they are caused by the devil, who stirs up such useless feelings in order to deceive us.

2. Such feelings, however, are sometimes very useful, for they stimulate our spiritual appetite, strengthen our spirit and help us to practise devotion with that holy joy and cheerfulness which adds grace and charm even to our exterior actions. David refers to the delight we may find in devotion when he says: *Meat most appetising are thy promises, O Lord, never was honey so sweet to my taste.*[1] Certainly the least spiritual consolation is worth far more than the greatest worldly pleasure; the milk from the breasts of the divine spouse is sweeter to the soul than the most costly wine of earthly pleasures;[2] once tasted, all other consolations are but gall. Those who taste liquorice find it so refreshing that they feel neither hunger nor thirst; so those who have tasted the heavenly manna of spiritual consolation neither hunger nor thirst earthly consolations, at least not to the extent of setting their heart on them. They are but foretastes of eternal happiness which God gives to those who seek him; the sugar plums by which he attracts his little ones; the health-giving waters by which he strengthens them; the pledges of their immortality.

It is said that Alexander the Great, sailing the high seas, was guided to Arabia Felix by the sweet perfumes carried from it by the wind, giving him and his companions fresh courage; so, on the sea of life, those

---

[1] Ps. 118. 103.   [2] Cf. Cant. 1.1.

feelings of sweetness and pleasure come to us as a foretaste of that heavenly land which we seek and to which we journey.

3. But, you may say, since some consolations are good and come from God whereas others are useless, dangerous and even evil, arising from our fallen nature or sent by the devil, by what means may we distinguish them one from the other? The answer is, Philothea, *You will know them by the fruit they yield.*[1] Our hearts are as trees, our feelings and desires their branches, our actions which follow from them the fruit; that heart is good which has good desires, those feelings are good which produce good effects and good actions. If feelings of pleasure, tenderness and consolation make us more humble and patient, considerate and merciful towards our neighbour, more fervent in mortifying our evil desires and inclinations, more constant in our devotion, more docile and submissive to those in authority over us, more simple in our lives, there can be no doubt that they come from God; but if we seek such feelings for our own satisfaction, if they make us selfish, irritable, self-assertive, impatient, overbearing, proud, presumptuous and harsh towards others and make us imagine that we are already saints and no longer in need of guidance or correction, there is no doubt that they are false and evil, for *a sound tree will* only *bear good fruit.*[2]

4. Such feelings and consolations must be received as follows:

(i) We must humble ourselves profoundly before God and never say on account of such feelings, "Oh, how good I am." No, Philothea, for such consolations, however good, do not make us any better than we are;

---

[1] Matt. 7. 16.   [2] Matt. 7. 17.

as I have said before, such feelings are not devotion. Let us rather say: *In God be thy trust, for him thy heart's longing, gracious thou shalt find him.*[1] When we eat sugar we cannot say that our mouth is sweet but only that the sugar is sweet, so while spiritual sweetness is good and God who gives it is good, it does not follow that those who receive it are good.

(ii) We must realize that we are still but little children in need of milk, and that these sugar plums are given to us because we are so frail and weak that we need to be enticed and attracted to the love of God.

(iii) Then, generally speaking, we must receive such gracious favours with humility and value them highly, so much because they are good in themselves but rather because they come from God, who, like a mother to please her little one, feeds it with sugar plums. If the child could understand it would derive more pleasure from the sweetness of its mother's loving tenderness and care than from the sweetness of the sugar plums; Philothea, while such feelings are sweet, the sweetest thing of all is to realize the loving and fatherly care of God who places them in our heart and mind and soul.

(iv) Having thus received them we must take care to use them according to the intention of him who gave them to us. Why does God grant us such feelings? In order to make us gentle towards others and loving towards himself. A mother gives sugar plums to win her child's caress, let us then caress our Lord when he gives us such feelings of sweetness, and embrace him tenderly, in other words, let us obey him, keep his commandments, do his will, seek to please him, and always be faithful and obedient. Such spiritual consolations, then,

[1] Lam. 3. 25.

should make us particularly careful to do good and practise humility.

(v) We must occasionally detach ourselves from such feelings of consolation, sweetness and tenderness by protesting to God that, though we accept them with loving humility as coming from him and because they help us to love him more, we seek only that love, not the sensible feelings. We should protest that we seek, not the consolation, but him who consoles; not the sweetness, but the source of that sweetness; not the tenderness, but him who is the joy of heaven and earth. Constant in these dispositions we must persevere in the love of God even though our whole lives are devoid of consolation, and be as ready on Mount Calvary as on Mount Tabor to say, *"Lord, it is well that we should be here with thee"*;[1] as ready to be with him on the cross as with him in glory.

(vi) Should you experience an abundance of such consolations or any extraordinary feelings of tenderness, compassion and sweetness, I strongly advice you to make this known to your confessor that you may learn how to moderate them and make best use of them; for it is written: *If thou find honey, eat thy fill and no more.*[2]

14. SPIRITUAL DESOLATION

ACT as I have advised you, Philothea, when you have consolations but remember that, like fair weather, such pleasures do not last, and that you will sometimes find yourself desolate and deprived of all feelings of devotion; your soul will seem like an arid desert, a barren

[1] Cf. Matt. 17. 4.   [2] Prov. 25. 16.

land, where there is no path to God, no refreshing waters of grace, but rather a drought which turns it into a waste land. In such a state, especially when extreme, we deserve every compassion, for then, like David, *morning and evening our diet is of tears*,[1] while the devil seeks to lead us to despair by countless mocking suggestions, saying, for example: "O wretched creature, *where is thy God now?*[2] By what road can you find him now? Who can ever restore the joy of his grace?"

What must we do at such a time, Philothea? The first thing is to discover the source of this evil, for often the cause of this desolation lies in ourselves.

1. A mother refuses sugar to a child subject to worms; so God withdraws his consolations when he sees that we take pleasure in them and are subject to the worms of vanity: *It was in mercy thou didst chasten me, schooling me to thy obedience; for idly I strayed till thou didst chasten me.*[3]

2. When, through sloth on our part, such consolations fail to bear fruit, he punishes us by taking them away. We find ourselves like those Israelites who, having failed to gather the manna before dawn, found it melted away after sunrise.

3. Like the bride in the Canticle of Canticles we sometimes rest on a bed of sensible consolation and when the spouse of our soul knocks on the door of our heart and calls us to the practice of devotion, we delay, unwilling to deprive ourselves of our false feeling of contentment and satisfaction, so that he passes on, and leaves us to our laziness; then, when we wish to seek him, he is hard to find. This is only what we deserve, having been faithless and disloyal to his love by prefer-

---

[1] Ps. 41.4.   [2] Ibid.   [3] Ps. 118. 71. 67.

233

ring to follow the things of the world. You cannot cling to the flour of Egypt and still have the manna of heaven. The delights of the Holy Spirit are incompatible with the artificial delights of the world.

4. Lack of frankness and sincerity with our confessor often causes spiritual desolation, for if you lie to the Holy Spirit it is not surprising if he refuses you his consolation. If you are not simple and sincere as a little child you will not receive any sugar plums.

5 If you have sated yourself with worldly pleasures it is not surprising that you have lost your taste for those of the spirit. "Doves already sated", says an ancient proverb, "find cherries bitter." *He has filled the hungry with good things*, says our Lady, *and sent the rich away empty-handed*;[1] those who are rich in worldly pleasures are not disposed for spiritual ones.

6. Have you carefully preserved the fruits of the consolations you have already received? If so, you will receive more. *If a man is rich, gifts will be made to him, and his riches will abound; if he is poor* (in other words, if, through his own fault he has lost what he has already been given), *even the little he has will be taken from him*,[2] for he will be deprived of the graces that were prepared for him.

Rain can revive plants which still have some leaves, but if they are leafless it destroys all further growth for it rots them completely.

If you have lost the consolations of devotion and fallen into spiritual dryness and desolation, examine your conscience and see if you have been guilty of some such defects as these. You must not, however, make this examination with anxiety or scrupulosity. If, after

[1] Luke 1. 53.   [2] Matt. 13. 12.

careful consideration, you find the cause of the evil in yourself, thank God, for evil is half cured once one has discovered its cause; if, on the contrary, you can find no particular cause for this dryness, spend no more time on further examination, but carry out the following advice in all simplicity:

(i) Conscious of your nothingness and wretchedness, humble yourself profoundly before God, saying, for example: "See what I am, my Saviour, left to myself: an arid and parched land, thirsting for the rain from heaven, windswept and reduced to dust."

(ii) Pray that God may grant you his joy: *Give me back the comfort of thy saving power.*[1] *My Father, if it is possible, let this chalice pass me by.*[2] Depart, O barren north wind that dries up my soul; come, O gentle wind of consolation, and *blow through this garden of mine,*[3] that the perfume of my desires may be shed abroad.

(iii) Open your heart to your confessor, revealing your soul to its very depths, then follow his advice with great simplicity and humility, such obedience being very dear to God, who often renders such counsels fruitful even though they may not appear very likely to prove useful, just as he cured Naaman by using the waters of the Jordan in which Eliseus had, seemingly without reason, ordered him to bathe.

(iv) Beyond all this, the best thing you can do is remain indifferent to deliverance from your spiritual desolation. This does not mean that you may not *wish* for this deliverance, but you must not *set your heart* on it. We must resign ourselves to God's merciful providence in our regard, prepared to serve him in the midst of these desert thorns as long as it pleases him. At such

---

[1] Ps. 50. 14.   [2] Matt. 26. 39.   [3] Cant. 4. 16.

times, then, let us say to God, *My Father, if it is possible, let this chalice pass me by*; but let us add courageously: *only as thy will is, not as mine is*;[1] preserving such resignation as long as possible. God will reward this holy indifference with many graces and favours, as he comforted Abraham with a consoling vision and many blessings when he saw that he was ready to sacrifice his son Isaac. Therefore, Philothea, whatever affliction, whether physical or spiritual, and whatever spiritual desolation we may be called upon to bear, we must say with all our heart and with complete surrender: "The Lord gave me consolations and the Lord has taken them away; blessed be the name of the Lord."[2] He will reward such humility, as he rewarded Job, by restoring his favours.

(v) Finally, Philothea, in the midst of our spiritual dryness and desolation let us remain courageous, and, while waiting patiently for the return of consolation, preserve the even tenor of our way, omitting none of our spiritual exercises, but rather, if possible, performing even more. If we cannot offer our Lord a devotion that is sweet let us offer him one that is dry, for it is all one to him so long as we are firmly resolved to love him. In fine spring weather the bees make more honey, yet produce fewer young ones, for they are so busy gathering honey from the flowers in the sunshine that they forget about them; but if the spring is cold and cloudy they produce more young ones and gather less honey; unable to go out and gather honey they thus employ themselves at home.

If often happens, Philothea, in the fair spring-time of spiritual consolations, we become so absorbed in

[1] Matt. 26, 39.   [2] Cf. Job. 1. 1.

their abundant delights that we perform fewer good works; on the contrary, in the midst of spiritual dryness and desolation, finding ourselves deprived of pleasure in devotion, we perform more good works and produce more abundant fruit through the interior practice of penance, humility, self-contempt, resignation, and renunciation of self-love.

Many, especially women, make the great mistake of thinking that their service of God is less pleasing to him when performed without sensible feelings of tenderness and satisfaction; on the contrary, our actions are like roses which are more graceful when fresh yet more fragrant when dry: they are more self-satisfying when performed with feelings of tenderness yet they are more precious to God, and their perfume is more sweet, when performed in a state of desolation. At such times, Philothea, we must *force* ourselves to serve God, and so our will must be more vigorous and constant than in times of consolation. It is no great thing to serve a prince in the quiet days of peace and amid the pleasures of the court; but to serve him amid the hardships of war, amid trouble and persecution, is a proof of constancy and fidelity.

Blessed Angela of Foligno says that the prayer which is most acceptable to God is that which we force ourselves to make, in other words, the prayers to which we apply ourselves, not because we find it attractive or because it is according to our inclinations, but simply to please God, the prayer which we force ourselves to make in spite of any dryness or repugnance we may feel.

The same applies to all good works; the more difficulties, whether exterior or interior, that we experience in doing them the more pleasing and precious are they in the sight of God, for the less there is of self-love in our acts of virtue the more the purity of divine love shines forth in them. A child readily kisses his mother when she gives him sugar but the true proof of his love is if he kisses her after she has given him a dose of some bitter medicine.

15. AN EXCELLENT EXAMPLE

To illustrate and clarify the above teaching here is an extract from a sound and learned life of St Bernard.

"Beginners in the service of God, unused to the withdrawal of sensible devotion, or the vicissitudes of the spiritual life, usually falter, lose courage and grow sad when deprived of the consolations and enlightenment which had made them hasten on their way to God. Experienced persons explain this by saying that human nature is unable to remain for any length of time without some kind of consolation, either heavenly or earthly. Lifted above ourselves, by tasting the pleasures of the spirit, we readily renounce those of earth, but if God then withdraws these spiritual joys, having already deprived ourselves of earthly consolation, and being as yet unaccustomed to wait patiently for the return of the true sun, we seem to be neither in heaven nor on earth but enveloped in everlasting night; then, like children weaned from the breast, we languish, lament and fret and become troublesome especially to ourselves."

Geoffrey of Péronne, who had only recently dedicated himself to the service of God, was travelling with St Bernard when he suddenly found himself in a state of spiritual dryness; deprived of consolation and overwhelmed with interior darkness he began to think of his worldly friends, of his relatives and of all the riches he had just forsaken, and was so tempted to sadness that he was unable to hide his feelings. One of his most intimate friends, on seeing this, took him aside and asked him gently, "What is the matter, Geoffrey? Why are you so pensive and sad, unlike your usual self?" With a deep sigh Geoffrey answered, "Ah, my friend, I shall never again be joyful." Moved to pity by these words and filled with concern, his friend went at once to their spiritual father, St Bernard, and told him about it. He, perceiving the danger, entered a nearby church and prayed for him. In the meantime, Geoffrey, overcome by sadness, lay down with his head upon a stone and fell asleep; after a while both rose up, St Bernard from his knees with his prayer answered, the other from his sleep with a face so smiling and serene that his friend, amazed at so great and sudden a change, could not help reproaching him a little for what he had said. Geoffrey answered him by saying, "If I told you a short while ago that I should never be happy again, I tell you now that I shall never be sad again!"

His temptation was thus brought to a successful issue, but in this story, Philothea, notice the following points:

1. That God usually gives a foretaste of heavenly delights to those who enter his service to detach them from earthly pleasures and encourage them in the pursuit of divine love, like a mother who honeys her breasts to entice her child.

2. That it is this same God who sometimes, in his wise providence, deprives us of the milk and honey of consolations so that, having been weaned, we may learn

to eat the dry but more solid food of a vigorous devotion exercised in the midst of dryness and temptation.

3. That sometimes great storms arise in the midst of such desolation. At such times we must fight constantly against temptations, for these do not come from God; but we must bear patiently with the sense of dryness as ordained by God for our advancement.

4. That we must never lose courage in the midst of such interior sufferings or say like Geoffrey: "I shall never be happy again"; for in the night we must await the dawn. On the other hand no matter how fair the weather in our spiritual life we must not say, "I shall never experience sorrow again," for as the wise man says: *Bethink thyself of foul weather in fair.*[1] In time of trial we must have hope; in time of prosperity, fear; while at all times we must be humble.

5. That the best remedy is to reveal our troubles to some spiritual friend who can console us.

To conclude this important advice I would remind you that in this matter, as in all others, God and the devil seek contrary ends; for God wishes by these trials to lead us to a greater purity of heart, to a complete renunciation of self-interest in his service and to perfect self-denial; but the devil wishes to make us lose courage, return to earthly pleasures and become a burden to ourselves and others. If, however, you carry out my advice and practise virtue in the midst of all these interior afflictions you will make great progress in perfection, but before concluding I must add a few more words with regard to these afflictions. Sometimes these feelings of distaste, dryness and desolation arise from some physical indisposition as when, for example,

[1] Ecclus. 11. 27.

we find ourselves oppressed with tiredness, drowsiness and fatigue through some excess in watching, labouring or fasting, which not only weary the body but the soul as well, by reason of the intimate relation between them. On such occasions we must make valiant acts of virtue with our superior will, for though our whole soul may seem to be asleep and oppressed with drowsiness and fatigue, such actions will be very pleasing to God and we can say at such a time with the Sacred Spouse, *I lie asleep; but oh, my heart is wakeful.*[1] Though, as I have already said, such acts are less pleasing to us, they are nevertheless more meritorious. The remedy on such occasions is to refresh the body by some lawful recreation and relaxation. St Francis made it a rule that his disciples should use such moderation in their labours as not to quench their ardour. He himself was once afflicted and troubled by so deep a sadness that he could not hide it; if he wished to speak to his companions he found he could not do so; if he withdrew from their company he felt worse; abstinence and mortification of the flesh merely oppressed him and he could find no relief even in prayer. This state lasted for two years so that he seemed altogether abandoned by God; but at last, after he had endured this violent storm with humility, our Lord in a single moment restored his joyful tranquillity. This shows that even the greatest servants of God experienced these trials and so we, who are the least of God's servants, should not be surprised if we experience them too.

[1] Cant. 5. 2.

PART FIVE

RENEWAL AND PRESERVATION OF DEVOTION

1. INTRODUCTION

THE following spiritual exercises are designed to renew and confirm our resolution to embrace the devout life. The first thing is to be convinced of their importance.

We are so frail and so weighed down by our evil inclinations that we only too easily fall away from our high purposes unless we often renew our good resolutions, like birds who fall to the ground unless they use their wings to maintain themselves in flight.

We must then, Philothea, renew time and time again our resolutions to serve God lest we fall back, not only to our former state but to a state worse than the first,[1] for this is what always happens when we fall back in the spiritual life.

No matter how good a clock may be it must be wound up repeatedly and overhauled every year for cleaning, for repairing parts that have become defective, and replacing those that are worn out. Our heart must be, as it were, wound up twice a day by morning and evening prayers and often examined, re-adjusted and corrected; it should be stripped at least once a year so that all its desires and inclinations may be examined in detail and any defects remedied.

A watchmaker uses fine oil to preserve the mechanism from rust and make it run more smoothly; we should do

[1] Cf. Luke 11. 26.

the same with our heart, after having overhauled it, by means of confession and Holy Communion, and thus renew its strength which time may have impaired, make it more fervent, freshen its resolves, renew its virtues and make them flourish. St Gregory Nazianzen tells us that the early Christians used diligently to renew their baptismal promise on the anniversary of our Lord's baptism; let us gladly follow their example, Philothea, and with a like diligence.

Having consulted your confessor, choose a suitable time and having secured for yourself a greater solitude than usual, both interior and exterior, make two or three meditations, in the way I have already described, on the following points.

2. THE VALUE OF YOUR RESOLUTION

1. CONSIDER the points of your resolution: first that you have forsaken, rejected, detested and renounced all mortal sin for ever; secondly that you have dedicated and consecrated your body, heart and soul and all your faculties to the love and service of God; thirdly that you have promised, with the help of God's grace, to rise again at once should you ever fall into sin. Enter into your soul and consider deeply how beautiful, noble and generous are such holy, reasonable and desirable resolves.

2. Consider to whom you made this resolution, for it was to God. If we are strictly bound by the promises we make to men how much more are we bound by those we make to God! As David said, *True to my heart's promise, I have eyes only for thee; be thy covenant ever in my thoughts, thy words kept in memory.*[1]

[1] Ps. 26. 8; 118. 16.

3. Consider in whose presence you made your resolution, for it was made in the sight of the very court of heaven; our Lady, St Joseph, your guardian angel, St Louis, the whole company of the blessed, approved your words with sighs of joy, and gazed on you with unspeakable love when they saw you prostrate yourself at the feet of our Lord and consecrate yourself to his service. Such joy in heaven will be renewed as, with all your heart, you now renew your resolution.

4. Consider what led you to make your protestation, and how gentle and gracious God was to you at the time, drawing you on by the attraction of the Holy Spirit. Did he not guide your little barque to the safe harbour *with leading-strings of love*[1] and charity? Consider how gently he drew you on by his grace, by the sacraments, by spiritual reading and by prayer; while you were asleep, Philothea, he was watching over you, thinking lovingly of your welfare.[2]

5. Consider when it was that God inspired you to make this resolution for it was in the prime of your life. What joy to know already what we can never know soon enough! St Augustine, converted at the age of thirty, cried out: "Late I have loved thee. O beauty so ancient and yet so new." May you not say in your turn: "O ancient sweetness, why have I tasted thee so late"? Alas, before, you did not deserve it; so now, recognizing the great favour that God has shown you in drawing you to himself in your youth, say with David, *It is thou, O God, that inspired me ever since the days of my youth, and still I am found telling the tale of thy wonders.*[3] If he had called you in your old age, after a misspent life, that too, Philothea, would have been a great grace;

[1] Osee 11. 4.   [2] Cf. Jer. 29. 11.   [3] Ps. 70. 17.

calling you before your death and turning you from a course of wretchedness which, had it continued, would have led you to eternal misery.

6. Consider the effects of your resolution; compare yourself now with what you were and I am sure you will find a change for the good. Is it not a blessing to know how to pray, to desire to love God, to have mastered your passions and tranquillized your soul, to have avoided so much sin and remorse and above all to have gone so much more often to Holy Communion, thus uniting yourself to the very fountainhead of eternal life? Such wonderful favours must be weighed, Philothea, in the scales of the sanctuary, for this is the work of God's right hand. As David says: *The power of the Lord has brought me great honour, the power of the Lord has triumphed. I am reprieved from death, to live on and proclaim what the Lord has done for me,*[1] with all my heart, in all my words and in all my actions.

After all these considerations, which should inspire you with many good desires, end quite simply, with an act of thanksgiving and a prayer that you may draw great profit from them. Then retire with humility and great confidence in God, reserving the task of making your resolutions until you have carried out the following exercises.

3 · EXAMINATION OF CONSCIENCE

THIS exercise is rather long, but remember that there is no need to go through it all at once; examine at one time, for example, your conduct towards God, at another your duty to yourself and the state of your in-

[1] Ps. 117. 16, 17.

clination, at another your conduct towards your neighbour.

It is not necessary nor expedient to kneel except for prayer at the beginning and the end. You can easily make your examination while out walking, perhaps more easily still in bed, so long as you can remain sufficiently awake for long enough. In this case, however, you should have read through the necessary considerations before retiring, and aim at completing the whole of this exercise within three days at the most, setting aside some convenient time each day, for it will lose its efficacy if too long protracted.

Having examined yourself on a particular point, note your failures, defects and principal disorders that you may confess them, and receive advice and strength in your resolve to amend.

It is not necessary to withdraw from company entirely while carrying out these exercises but you should do so to a certain extent, especially towards evening, retiring early to take the bodily and spiritual repose so necessary for meditation.

During the day make frequent aspirations to God, our Lady, and to the angels, in fact, to all the citizens of the heavenly Jerusalem, your heart filled with love of God and a desire for your spiritual perfection.

To begin your examination properly place yourself in the presence of God and invoke the Holy Spirit that he may enlighten you and enable you to see yourself clearly as you really are, praying humbly with St Augustine, "Teach me to know thee, O Lord, and to know myself"; or saying with St Francis, "Who art thou, O Lord, and who am I?" Protest that you wish to note your progress, not for your own satisfaction but to

rejoice in it for God's sake; not for your own glory but
for his, that you may thank him. Protest also, if you
seem to have made little progress or even fallen back,
that you will not give way to discouragement and become faint-hearted and lukewarm, but on the contrary
that you will stir yourself to greater efforts, humble
yourself and strive with God's grace to remedy your
defects. Having done this, consider calmly and peacefully how you have behaved up to the present towards
God, your neighbour and yourself.

4. YOUR BEHAVIOUR TOWARDS GOD

1. WHAT is your attitude towards mortal sin? Are you
firmly resolved to avoid it at all costs? Have you kept
this resolution since you embraced the devout life?
Remember that it is its very foundation.

2. What is your attitude towards God's commandments? Do you find them good, delightful and attractive? Those whose taste is good, and whose stomachs
are healthy, enjoy good food and reject what is bad.

3. What is your attitude towards venial sin? We cannot avoid this altogether but are you inclined to any
particular venial sin, or, what is worse, attached to it?

4. What is your attitude towards spiritual exercises?
Do you love and value them or do you find them
wearisome and distasteful? To which do you feel more
or less inclined? Do you feel any repugnance in listening
to or reading or discussing the word of God, in meditating, making aspirations, going to confession, receiving
spiritual advice, preparing for and receiving Holy
Communion, or in keeping a watch over your heart? If

you discover any such disinclination, find out the root and cause of your distaste.

5. What is your attitude towards God himself? Do you take pleasure and delight in thinking of him, like David who said, *It is to God my thoughts turn, in him lies all my content?*[1] Do you experience any facility for loving God, and does this love bring you satisfaction? Does it bring you peace to think of the immensity, goodness and sweetness of God? If the memory of God comes to you amid your worldly occupations, does it find a ready welcome? Does it possess your heart? Does your heart seem to turn towards God and, as it were, go to meet him, as certainly happens in some cases?

When a woman's husband returns from a long journey, as soon as she hears his voice and knows that he is home, even though she may be busily engaged in some occupation which she cannot leave, her thoughts turn at once to him and her heart goes out to meet him. It is the same with those who love God; no matter how busy they may be, as soon as the memory of God returns, they find it so delightful that they give little heed to anything else; and this is a very good sign.

6. What is your attitude towards Jesus Christ, true God and true Man? Do you delight in him as bees in honey? or are you like the wasps who delight in garbage? For the good find all their happiness in Christ, and love him most tenderly; but the wicked find happiness only in futilities.

7. What is your attitude towards our Lady, the saints, your guardian angel? Have you a great love for them? Do you take pleasure in their pictures, in praising them, and in reading their lives?

[1] Ps. 76. 4.

8. How do you speak of God? Do you delight in speaking well of him as far as you are able in your state of life? Do you love to sing his praises?

9. Have you a sincere desire to do all you can to promote the external glory of God and his honour? Those who love God *love the beauty of his house.*[1]

10. Can you remember having gone against any inclination or given up anything for God's sake? For it is a true proof of love to give up something for the sake of the beloved.

5. YOUR BEHAVIOUR TOWARDS YOURSELF

1. IN what way do you love yourself? Is it largely for the sake of this world? If this is the case you will desire to remain here always and take every care to make yourself secure on earth. If it is for the sake of heaven, you will desire or at least be ready to leave this world whenever it shall please our Lord.

2. Is your life well ordered? For it is only inordinate love of self which leads to our own ruin. A well-ordered love demands that we should love the soul more than the body, should be more anxious to acquire virtue then anything else and set greater store on our glory in heaven than on the transitory glory of this world, saying to ourselves, not "What will men say?" but "What will the angels think?"

3. What sort of love have you for your heart? With what care do you seek to cure it in its infirmities? It is your duty to do all you can for it when it is tormented by passions and to lay all else aside to bring it relief.

[1] Ps. 25. 8.

4. What do you count yourself in the sight of God? Doubtless, nothing. Now there is not much humility in a fly counting itself nothing compared with a mountain, nor in a drop of water counting itself nothing compared with the sea, nor in a little spark counting itself nothing compared with the sun; true humility lies in not counting ourselves more estimable than others and in not wishing that others should count us so. How do you stand in this respect?

5. How do you talk about yourself? Are you boastful and conceited?

6. Do you indulge in any pleasures detrimental to your health, in other words, pleasures which are useless and futile, for example, too many late nights without any good reason, and so on?

6. YOUR BEHAVIOUR TOWARDS YOUR NEIGHBOUR

THE love of husband and wife for one another should be sweet and tranquil, and such is God's will. The same applies in due order to children, close relatives and friends. What is your attitude in general to those about you? Do you love them with all your heart for God's sake? To answer this properly consider those whom you find disagreeable and tedious, for it is in such cases that we most clearly practise fraternal love, and above all in the case of those who harm us either in word or deed. Examine carefully whether you are well disposed towards them or whether you find it hard to love them. Are you ready to speak ill of your neighbour, especially of those who dislike you? Do you do anything to harm your neighbour either directly or indirectly? A little reflection will soon make this clear.

7. AN EXAMINATION OF YOUR GENERAL
DISPOSITIONS

BECAUSE the knowledge of your spiritual progress depends upon the examination of the above points, I have treated of them at length; to restrict your examination to sins alone is to be like those who go to confession without any real desire to make progress.

Take these points quite peacefully, one at a time, and consider the state of your heart in their regard since you made your resolution, noting any serious faults. If a detailed examination such as I have suggested would prove too laborious it may be simplified and reduced to a scrutiny of your passions as follows:

What have been your dispositions and how have you acted with regard to:

1. Your love of God, your neighbour and yourself.

2. Your hatred of your own sins and those of others; for in both cases we should desire their extirpation.

3. Your desire for possessions, pleasures and honours.

4. Your fear of the occasions of sin and your fear of temporal loss. We fear the former too little and the latter too much.

5. Your hope, set, perhaps, too much on the world and on created things and not enough on God and on eternal things.

6. Your sadness; perhaps too excessive over unimportant matters.

7. Your joy; perhaps too excessive over unworthy matters.

In other words, what inclinations sway your heart? What passions possess it? Where has it gone most astray? Test the passions of your soul one by one and you will know its state. A lute player having tested the strings of his lute tightens or loosens them when he finds them out of tune; so, having tested the passions of your soul, its love and its hate, its desire, fear and hope, its sadness and joy, you should likewise tune them, if necessary, by means of God's grace and the advice of your confessor, that you may play the melody you desire, which is the praise of God's glory.

8. SPIRITUAL ACTS IN CONCLUSION

HAVING quietly completed your examination and discovered the state of your soul, conclude with the following spiritual acts:

1. Thank God for any progress you have made since your resolution, acknowledging that it is entirely due to his mercy.

2. Humble yourself profoundly before God, acknowledging that if this progress is scanty it is entirely due to your lack of fidelity, courage and constancy in corresponding with his graces and inspirations.

3. Promise to praise him eternally for the graces which have enabled you to overcome your evil inclinations and make progress, no matter how slight.

4. Ask pardon for having been so unfaithful and disloyal to grace.

5. Offer him your soul that he may be its sole master.

6. Beg him to make you completely faithful to him.

7. Invoke the saints, our Lady, your guardian angel, your patron saint, St Joseph, and so on.

9. CONSIDERATIONS ON RENEWING YOUR RESOLUTION

HAVING completed the above, and having discussed your defects and their remedies with your confessor, make each of the following considerations the subject of your daily meditation, following the method I have already explained, placing yourself first of all in the presence of God and praying for grace to establish you firmly in his love and service.

10. FIRST CONSIDERATION: THE EXCELLENCE OF YOUR SOUL

CONSIDER the nobility and excellence of your soul; endowed with reason, it not only knows this visible world but also knows that there is a heaven, that there are angels, that there is a God and that he is supreme, ineffable and good; reason which knows that there is an eternity and understands how to live in this world in order to live for ever in company with God and his angels in the next.

Your soul is also endowed with a most noble will capable of loving God and incapable of hating him in himself. Consider how great is your heart which can find no rest except in God and which nothing created can ever satisfy, like the bees that are attracted by nothing corrupt but rest only upon the flowers. Remember quite freely the most perfect delight which your heart has so far experienced. If you are honest you must admit that in the midst of such delight your heart was still miserable, full of disquiet, cares and anxieties. Our heart tends to seek created things, eagerly thinking that they will satisfy its desires, but once it has attained them it sees that it is back where it started, and that nothing in this world can satisfy it. God does not will that it should find rest on earth; he wills that it should return to him from whom it went forth, like the dove which Noe sent forth from the ark. Why, when our heart has been endowed with such beauty by nature, do we divert it from its true inclination and make it serve created things? "O my beautiful soul", you should say, "why, when you can know and love God, are you occupied with something less? Why, when you can aspire to eternity, are you taken up with the passing moments of time?"

One of the things which the prodigal son most regretted was that, when he might have been eating delightful food at his father's table, he had been eating husks with swine. "O my soul, what wretchedness, when you can enjoy God, to be content with anything less." Lift up your soul in this way; realize that it is eternal and worthy of eternity; stir up your courage to attain this end.

II. SECOND CONSIDERATION: THE EXCELLENCE OF THE VIRTUES

CONSIDER that nothing but virtue and devotion can bring you happiness in this world. Consider the beauty of the virtues compared with their contrary vices. How beautiful is patience compared with revenge; gentleness compared with anger and acrimony; humility compared with pride and ambition; generosity compared with avarice; charity compared with envy; moderation compared with dissipation! Virtues have the admirable quality of filling the soul with incomparable sweetness and delight when they are practised, whereas vices leave the soul completely weary, and dissatisfied. Why not strive then for such delight?

If we have a few vices we are not content; if we have more, we are more discontented than ever; on the other hand even a few virtues bring us some degree of contentment and the more we advance in virtue, the more this contentment grows. Oh how beautiful, how delightful, how pleasing and agreeable is the devout life! It lightens our troubles, and makes consolations more sweet; but without devotion our good is turned to ill, and our pleasures are full of disquiet, trouble and disappointment. Those who know the value of devotion might well exclaim with the woman of Samaria: *Lord, give me this water,*[1] an aspiration frequently used by St Teresa and St Catherine of Genoa, though in different senses.

12. THIRD CONSIDERATION: THE EXAMPLE OF THE SAINTS

CONSIDER the example of all the various saints; what have they not done in their love and service of God? Consider the invincible fidelity of the martyrs, and the torments they endured to keep their resolution. Consider above all those women, their beauty in full bloom, whiter than the lily in purity, redder than the rose in charity, who, some at the age of twelve, others at the age of thirteen, fifteen, twenty or twenty-five, suffered countless forms of martyrdom rather than renounce their resolutions, not only with regard to their faith, but

[1] John 4. 15.

also with regard to their devotion; some choosing to die rather than forsake their virginity, others rather than give up serving the sick, comforting the afflicted or burying the dead. What constancy the weaker sex has shown on such occasions! Consider the many holy confessors and with what fortitude they despised the things of the world. They too were invincible and nothing could make them weaken in their resolutions; having embraced them without reserve they kept them without faltering. Remember what St Augustine says of the steadfastness of his mother, St Monica, in carrying out her resolution to serve God both in her marriage and as a widow; St Jerome speaks in the same way of his spiritual daughter, Paula; and this was in the face of very great obstacles and in all sorts of circumstances. After such wonderful examples, what is there that we may not do? They were as we are; they did it for the same God and for the same virtues. Why should we not do as much, according to our state of life and our circumstances, in order to keep our cherished resolution and to fulfil our holy protestation?

13. FOURTH CONSIDERATION: CHRIST'S LOVE FOR US

CONSIDER the love with which our Lord Jesus Christ suffered so much in this world, above all in the Garden of Olives and on Mount Calvary. Consider that you were the object of this love; expressed in all this pain and suffering it obtained for you from God the Father the grace to embark on the devout life and to make your good resolutions; it obtained all the graces you need to maintain, strengthen and fulfil them. How precious, then, is your resolution, being the fruit of your Saviour's Passion. Consider how you should cherish what has been so dear to Jesus. "O my Saviour, you died to purchase for me the grace to make my resolutions; grant me the grace to die rather than forsake them." Remember, Philothea, that it is certain that our Lord beheld your heart and loved it as he hung upon the Cross, and by his love obtained for you all the good things you have ever had or ever will have, including your resolutions. Yes, Philothea, God says to us what he said to the prophet Jeremias: *I claimed thee for my own before ever I fashioned thee in thy mother's womb,*[1] for in his goodness, love and mercy he truly prepared all the means of our salvation, both general and particular, and consequently our good resolutions.

As a woman with child prepares the cradle, the linen and the swaddling clothes, even arranging for a nurse and everything necessary for the child she hopes to bring forth, so our Lord, his goodness, as it were, pregnant with you upon the Cross, wishing to bring you forth to salvation and make you his child, prepared everything you would need: your spiritual cradle, linen and swaddling clothes; your nurse and everything required for your happiness, in other words, all the means, all the attractions and graces by which he guides your soul and seeks to lead it to perfection.

How deeply this truth should be engraved upon our memory. "Is it possible, my Saviour, that you have loved me so tenderly and thought of me so particularly in all these little ways, by which you have drawn me to yourself? How greatly then should I love and cherish them; how carefully profit by them!"

[1] Cf. Jer. 1. 4.

How wonderful to realize, Philothea, that God has loved you and prepared countless means for your salvation as though you were the only person in the world to be considered, just as the sun shines on one part of the earth as brightly as though it shone nowhere else.

He loved me and gave himself for me,[1] says St Paul, speaking as though our Lord had done it for him alone. Imprint this truth, Philothea, on your very soul as a means of preserving and strengthening your resolution so precious to our Saviour's heart.

14. FIFTH CONSIDERATION: GOD'S ETERNAL LOVE FOR US

CONSIDER the eternal love which God has had for you. Before our Lord, as man, suffered for you on the Cross, as God, he knew and loved you in his infinite goodness. When did he begin to love you? When he began to be God? No, for he is without beginning and without end; he has always been God and so has loved you from eternity and in that love prepared all the graces and favours he has bestowed on you. He tells you so through the Prophet Jeremias in words addressed to you as though there were no one else: *With unchanging love I love thee, and now in mercy I have drawn thee to myself.*[2] Among other things he thought of drawing you to make your resolutions to serve him.

"How important these resolutions must be, my God, since you have thought of them, considered and designed them from all eternity! How dear and precious should they be to me! How much should I be prepared to

[1] Gal. 2. 20.   [2] Jer. 31. 3.

suffer rather than fail in the least of them! Rather should I let the whole world perish, for it is not worth my soul, and my soul is worth nothing without its resolutions."

15. GENERAL CONSIDERATIONS IN CONCLUSION

MY resolutions are the beautiful tree of life planted by God himself in my heart and watered by my Saviour's precious blood to make it bear fruit. I would rather undergo a thousand deaths than allow any storm to uproot this tree. No vanities, pleasures, riches nor afflictions shall divert me from my purpose.

"You have planted and preserved this beautiful tree in your fatherly Heart, my God, from all eternity, ready for my garden; and how many others have not been so favoured! How shall I ever humble myself enough before your mercy?"

How beautiful and sacred my resolutions; if I keep them they will keep me; as long as they live in my soul I too will live; may they live forever, then, as they have lived eternally in the mercy of my God, and may I never abandon them.

After these considerations, decide on the particular means necessary to fulfil your resolutions, protesting that you desire to make faithful use of them; such means for example as prayer, the frequentation of the sacraments, good works, the amendment of the faults you have discovered, the avoidance of the occasions of sin the practice of your confessor's advice, and so on.

Then, summoning up all your strength and fervour, make countless promises of fidelity to your resolution, dedicating, consecrating and sacrificing your whole being to God, protesting that you will never retract your offering, but leave yourself forever at the service of his holy will.

Ask God to regenerate your whole life and bless and strengthen your renewed resolve; invoke our Lady, your guardian angel, St Louis, and other saints.

In these dispositions go to your confessor, accuse yourself of the principal faults committed since your general confession, and, having received absolution, read and sign your protestation in his presence. Finally go to Holy Communion and unite yourself, thus renewed in spirit, to your Saviour, the source of all your life.

16. SENTIMENTS TO BE PRESERVED

ON the day you renew your resolution, and on the days following, make constant use of aspirations, as did St Paul, St Augustine, St Catherine of Genoa and others, saying, for example: "I am no longer my own; whether I live or die I belong to my Saviour." "I have nothing of my own, I belong to Jesus and all I have is his." "The world remains the same, as I have remained till now; but I will remain the same no longer; my heart is changed and the world which so often deceived me will be deceived in me; not noticing my gradual change, it will think of me as Esau when in reality I will have become Jacob."

These sentiments should rest quietly in your heart and you should pass from your considerations and meditation to your ordinary affairs and occupations gently, without straining either mind or body, lest you spill the precious balm of your resolutions before it has penetrated into the very depth of your soul.

17. AN ANSWER TO TWO OBJECTIONS

WORLDLY people will tell you, Philothea, that anyone who tries to put all these counsels and instructions into practice will have no time for anything else. Even if this were so we would be doing enough, Philothea, for we would be fulfilling our purpose in this world; but it is obviously a fallacy. It would be true if it were necessary to practise them all every day, but, in fact, it is only necessary to practise them as and when the occasion demands. Think of the innumerable laws in the civil code; they must all be observed but only when they apply, and this does not happen every day. King David used to practise far more spiritual exercises than I have advocated, despite the fact he was constantly occupied with very difficult affairs. St Louis, as great a king in peace as in war, and one who administered justice and managed his affairs with incomparable care, used to hear two Masses every day, say Vespers and Compline with his chaplain, make his meditation, visit the hospitals, and go to confession and take the discipline every Friday, frequently attend sermons and take part in spiritual discussions; yet he never wasted any opportunity of working for the public good, and fulfilled his public duties with every care, while his court was more splendid and flourishing than it had ever been in the time of his predecessors. Be courageous, then, Philothea, in putting all these instructions into practice as I have suggested and God will give you sufficient leisure and strength to fulfil all your duties, even though he should have to make the sun stand still as he did for Josue. We always do enough, when God works with us.

Worldly people will say that I nearly always presume the gift of mental prayer in a *Philothea*, whereas this is not always the case, so that this *Introduction* is not suitable for everyone. It is true that I have presumed this and it is also true that not everyone has the gift of mental prayer; nevertheless, there is no doubt that nearly all, even the most stupid, are capable of acquiring this gift, provided that they have a good spiritual director and are prepared to give it the attention it deserves. In the rare cases where this is not possible a wise director can easily teach them how to read through the meditations carefully, or to listen to them being read out, in such a way that they compensate for this defect.

18. FINAL ADVICE

RENEW your resolve on the first day of every month and at all times protest your determination to observe it, saying with David, *Life-giving are thy commands, O Lord, never to be forgotten.*[1] Should you experience any disorder in your soul, humble yourself upon your knees, your protestation in your hand, then read it through with heartfelt devotion and it will bring you relief. Confess openly that you wish to be devout; I say, that you *wish* to be devout, not that you *are* devout. Never be ashamed of taking the ordinary means necessary to progress in the love of God. Acknowledge quite frankly that you try to meditate and that you would rather die than fall into mortal sin; that you desire to frequent the sacraments and follow your confessor's advice; though often, for various reasons, there is no need to mention his name. This frank profession of our

[1] Ps. 118. 93.

desire to serve God and to consecrate ourselves whole-
heartedly to his love is most pleasing to our Lord, who
does not want us to be ashamed either of him or of his
Cross; moreover, such frankness serves to silence the
contrary suggestions of worldly people and commits us
in honour to live up to what we profess.

Philosophers used to proclaim themselves philosophers that they might be allowed to live as such;
so should we profess our desire to be devout that we
may be allowed to live devoutly. If anyone says that we
can live devoutly without practising all these exercises,
do not deny it, but answer quietly that you are so weak
that you need more help and assistance than others.

Finally, Philothea, by all that is sacred in heaven and
on earth, by your baptism, by the breasts which nourished your Saviour, by the heart with which he loves
you, by the infinite mercy in which you hope, by all
these things, I entreat you to continue and persevere
in the practice of the devout life. Our days pass away
and death is at the door. "The trumpet sounds the
retreat", says St Gregory Nazianzen, "let everyone be
ready, for the judgement is at hand." When the mother
of St Symphorian saw him being led away to martyrdom she cried after him: "My son, remember eternal
life; look up to heaven and think of him who reigns
there. Your approaching death will quickly end this
life's brief course." I say the same to you, Philothea:
look up to heaven and do not forsake it for anything on
earth; look down into hell and do not cast yourself there
for the sake of transitory things; look up to Jesus
Christ; do not deny him for the sake of the world, and
should the labours of the devout life seem hard to you,
sing with St Francis:

Because I seek eternity,
All labours here are light to me.

May Jesus reign, to whom, with the Father and the Holy Spirit, be honour and glory now and forever.

Amen.